Service:
Managing The
Guest Experience

Service: Managing The Guest Experience

Author
Donald I. Smith

Westin Distinguished Professor
Hotel and Restaurant Administration
College Of Business and Economics
Washington State University

Prepared for

The Educational Foundation of the National Restaurant Association Foodservice Manager Self-Development Program.

The Advisory Board for the Foodservice Manager Self-Development Program as reviewed this book and recommends it for use by members of the food industry.

Service: Managing The Guest Experience

10 9 8 7 6 5 4 3 2 1

Printed in the United States of America
Library of Congress Catalog Card Number: 87-073515
International Standard Book Number: 086730-253-4

Acknowledgements

There were many wonderful people who helped with this book, chief among them Charles Bernstein, the Publications Committee, and Sandie Meyers, Gladys Russell, and Helen Stevens, who translated my hieroglyphics, arrows, and Chicago grammar.

I also want to thank some of my teachers, each of whom made a profound impact on my knowledge of the restaurant business—a knowledge, understanding, and wisdom that I can now share with my students at Washington State University.

These superstars include:

Win Schuler, who taught me how to concentrate on people, remember their names and feed their self-esteem as well as their appetites.

Sonny Look, who made it clear that the restaurant business is show business and every night should be opening night.

Pete Harman, the most caring manager I ever met, who taught me that the care you show to your staff reflects itself in the care your staff gives to the guests.

Tony Athenas, a master of detail.

Ray Eliot, my coach, who was the embodiment of actions speaking louder than words.

My Uncle Rocco, who, in pungent language, made me aware of how pride, passion, and attention to detail in service and hospitality begins at the top with the manager.

My mother, who taught me the importance of giving the customer "the unexpected extra."

My wife and kids, who taught me how to listen—really listen.

Tom Drohan, Gretchen Gohlert, Teck-Meng Lim, Joe Reger, and Chris Teich—the 1987 senior class in Multi-Unit Management at Washington State University—who, in their study of twenty fast-service restaurants, validated the premise that the district manager and the unit manager made all the difference in activating and inspiring an exceptionally hospitable restaurant staff.

The wonderful Ivy Award-winning team at Chateau Louise in Chicago land who proved over thirteen years that customers not only notice exceptional service, but generate enormous numbers of new guests through word-of-mouth, conclusively demonstrating that hospitality is the key to positioning your restaurant as clearly superior to all others in its class.

Donald I. Smith

Preface

This is a book about the kind of restaurant service that makes customers and keeps customers the old-fashioned way—inside the restaurant. The restaurant manager's prime responsibility is to create loyal guests and repeat business the only way that really works in the long haul—one at a time. Building customer satisfaction by keeping the hot food hot and the cold food cold and at the same time being friendly under pressure is not an easy task under the best of circumstances. Add to this the need to cope with the changes that are now taking place in the industry, and you have a monumental undertaking.

The key is to develop caring service. In a word: hospitality.

If this book had been written for restaurant professionals of the 1960s and 1970s, the focus would have been on "concept development." This was the era of creative restaurant formulas, of special interior decoration, of planned policies, packaging, and decor. There was a fifteen-year period during which restaurants were differentiated primarily by location and ambiance, and although we offered our customers only a limited menu and impersonal service, the booming population continued to fill our establishments. As long as we were well located, consistent, and without surprises, it seemed to work.

During the 1980s, we have experienced another profound transition. Popular tastes and lifestyles have been constantly changing. The focus in restaurants shifted to food. We witnessed changes in taste, some brief fads, and some long-term trends. There was a move from cocktails to wine, from bland to spicy foods, and most of all, a nation of eaters and diners who were willing to experiment with taste much more than the previous generation. Thus, in food service guidelines, we have seen a transition from "Put your differentiation on the wall" to "Put it on your plate."

It's the 1990s consumer we will have to satisfy now. The new technology, demographics, and lifestyles are impacting the very nature of the food service industry. We are facing some profound changes in customer wants. Many of our prospects are finding more pleasure in staying at home with their VCRs and TVs and home-delivered deli meals than they are in dealing with the hassle and inconvenience of eating out.

We have too many restaurants chasing too few customers, and these old-formula restaurants are beginning to blur in the customer's mind. The menus, service, prices, and advertising are producing a depressing and discouraging sameness. We are now experiencing an attempt at differentiation by price promotion, with emphasis on TV advertising, special coupon sales, and the pushing of more trendy new food fads.

Today's customers are—and tomorrow's will be—older, more experienced, and greatly demanding. They expect food service that emphasizes restaurant "QSC"—quality food, efficient service, and comfortable surroundings. This means restaurateurs will need to plan well and work hard to rise above the competition.

The focus for the 1990s will be a shift from policy formulas to entrepeneurial spirit. There will be less emphasis on using marketing techniques to increase guest traffic and more emphasis on making and keeping customers through personalized caring service, which is the essence of hospitality. Decor, food, and promotion will continue to be important to success, but we are returning now to a business era where the top establishments will be those that have recognized the satisfied customer as their most precious commodity. We will be driven by the goal of repeat business, and the way we will best attain this will be through interacting in a caring way with the people who are our customers—the manager "working the floor," remembering the names of the guests, listening to them, and responding to all the little things that make such a great difference in customer satisfaction.

In this book, service is presented as (a) a user-friendly engineered system for delivering the product we call service; (b) a set of procedures for exceeding the expectations of the guests; and (c) a relationship between guest and restaurant staff that results in the guest wanting to return and repeat the pleasurable experience.

Managing the guest experience through service is what this book is all about.

Contents

1

Service: The Focus is on Guest Satisfaction

Caring Service Is in Demand

The concept of service is in the limelight. The media, business executives, and academics agree that the economy has shifted from manufacturing to service industries. Recent books, such as *Megatrends: Ten New Directions Transforming Our Lives, In Search of Excellence: Lessons from America's Best-run Companies,* and *Service America: Doing Business in the New Economy* have become best sellers. The terms *quality service, customer satisfaction,* and *excellence* are being explored by business people and academics as never before. Service has been rediscovered and appears more frequently than ever in industry mission statements, literature, and seminars.

Despite this acknowledgment of quality service as a competitive advantage, the public is asking "What service?" "Where's the quality?" Without hesitation, most consumers can recount a recent, frustrating ex-

1

perience with poor service or with products that did not perform as expected.

This country's economic strength has been founded on its ability to employ its vast resources, to innovate, and to mass produce. The current challenge and the one of the future will be its ability to muster its greatest resource, the human one, to provide caring, hospitable service. The fact is, the consumer wants service; but many business people are unfamiliar with efficient and effective ways to deliver it.

Today, because there are more business opportunities in the service sector, companies have no choice but to devote more energy to understanding and providing quality service. It is evident that those who are not quality-service oriented will lose out to those who are. (David Halberstam in his recent book, *The Reckoning: The Challenge to America's Greatness*, provides an example of how this has already occurred in the American automobile industry.) Consequently, businesses are searching for service strategies that work.

The restaurant industry has more experience with service strategies than most other industries. Service is the industry's mainstay, and it, along with food and atmosphere, are what its guests are buying. Guests cannot touch the quality service experience, but they feel its result and notice its absence. Thus, restaurant service can be defined as an intangible product of useful labor which provides a guest benefit.

The Three Components of Quality Service

Quality service has three primary components: (1) a distribution system; (2) a standard operating procedure for creating a memorable experience for the guest; and (3) a personal relationship between the guest and the restaurateur that results in the guest's desire to repurchase after a sale has been made.

- *Service as a distribution system.* Service is a technical or engineered system and style of distribution. It is based on effectively applying engineering principles that best satisfy guests' needs. It encompasses functions such as order taking, delivery, merchandising, billing, collecting, and so forth. Service delivery systems include self-service, cafeteria service, table service, drivethrough, delivery, and all the varieties of systems and styles within each of these categories. The service distribution system is the foundation upon which a restaurant builds an experience and shapes a relationship with its guests. Distribution systems for similar types of establishments can vary greatly based on a facility's service goals. For example, one fast-service restaurant may effectively use a scramble cuing system; while another finds that a serpentine line better meets its needs.

- *Service as a standard procedure for creating an exceeded expectation for the guest.* The service experience is the benefit that results from a set of planned and manageable procedures and policies, the sum of which causes guests to perceive that the restaurateur's product offers a competitive advantage. A guest experience is the sum of everything that management plans to make happen to a guest from arrival to departure. The service procedure must be managed, i.e., planned, executed, monitored, and evaluated. When service is managed properly, the guest leaves with a feeling of added satisfaction. This feeling generates a range of guest benefits, including trust and security, social gratification, ego enhancement, and, possibly, new knowledge. In return, the guest bestows upon the organization the benefits of capital generated by repeat visits, increased frequency of visits, and word-of-mouth advertising. For example, one famous pizza chain provides greater value through speed and convenience in its 30-minute guaranteed home delivery. As a result, it has carved out a new niche from what some had called a saturated market.

- *Service as a relationship between buyer and seller.* This is the human side of service. It is often described as *hospitality*—a set of interactive behaviors that is directed by the service employee toward the personal needs and wants of guests. The result of the relationship is to maximize the loyalty, trust, and respect of the guest for the restaurant. Hospitality, or caring service, creates a pleasant and friendly bond between guest and personnel. To provide hospitality, service personnel must have the necessary interpersonal skills and behaviors that generate positive verbal and non-verbal communication with the guest. These talents and skills are not taught. While they can be influenced and enhanced, there is no policy manual that can address the thousands of different situations that arise each day in a restaurant. The service person must instantaneously respond to a guest's comment or movement. Some people are endowed with service skills, while others are not. Producing a service relationship is dependent on an effective personnel recruitment and selection system, then, and only then, upon all the human resource functions, such as training, coaching, compensation, incentives, feedback, and grievance procedures.

All three service components are vital for a restaurant to provide quality service. When these components are effectively managed, they enable an organization to use service as a differentiation strategy, enabling it to stand out from all others. Although two restaurants might have identical menus, service systems, decor, prices, and reputations, a guest can leave one establishment elated, but leave the other one disappointed. Exceptional service is also a means of creating a competitive advantage by increasing the value-to-price benefit to guests.

Service is a rather unique product. Karl Albrecht and Ron Zemke, authors of *Service America: Doing Business in a New Economy*, believe service is different from all other products because (5):

- Service is produced at the instant of delivery; it cannot be created in advance or held in readiness.

- A service cannot be centrally produced, inspected, stockpiled, or warehoused. It is usually delivered wherever the customer is, by people who are beyond the immediate influence of management.

- The "product" cannot be demonstrated, nor can a sample be sent for customer approval in advance of the service.

- The experience itself cannot be sold or passed on to a third party.

- If improperly performed, a service cannot be "recalled." If it cannot be performed anew, then reparations or apologies are the only means of recourse for customer satisfaction.

- Quality assurance must happen *before* rather than *after* production, as would be the case in a manufacturing situation.

- Delivery of the service usually requires human interaction to some degree; buyer and seller come into contact in some relatively personal way to create the service.

- The guests' expectations of service are integral to their satisfaction with the outcome. Quality of service is largely a subjective matter.

- The more employees guests must encounter during service delivery, the less likely it is that they will be satisfied with the service.

In recent decades, many foodservice managers have focused on the engineering aspects of service, i.e., on delivery systems, styles, and techniques. Restaurateurs have looked to operational efficiencies to improve their profits and also provide convenience to their guests. The growth of fast-service establishments, technological changes, and growing labor costs in all types of facilities have contributed to the emphasis on this particular service component.

Service As a "Profit-maker"

Those who hold the traditional concept that service is solely a distribution system, approach service as a cost of doing business. They view service as an expense to control and reduce. They believe in the conventional wisdom that, "The lower the cost of service, the better." They measure service and state the result as a percentage of sales (which usually ranges from 16 to 33 percent of sales in commercial restaurants). However, a new view of service is emerging. It is being viewed not only as being a distribution system, but also as having a sales profit function. When service is performed effectively, the average guest check can be increased and profits optimized. In addition, if guests' expectations are exceeded, they are likely to return to the restaurant often and spread a positive word among friends and acquaintances. These increased visits or positive word-of-mouth (WOM) mean more business for the facility; more business means more potential profits.

The Profit Picture

Foodservice industry sales are growing, although not as quickly as in past years. The National Restaurant Association (NRA) forecasts moderate growth in sales in the near future (*13*). Chart 1.1 shows the industry's growth pattern; while Chart 1.2 shows the sales and growth rate for various industry segments. Chart 1.3 shows projected growth rate for 1987 by region. *Note:* Figures in these charts, and all others in this text, are based on industry averages. Figures in any particular chart may or may not reflect the actual picture for any given company or restaurant.

The profit picture for the foodservice industry is quite another story. For most foodservice categories, food costs have dropped, but the costs for utilities, labor, advertising and promotion, repairs and maintenance, supplies, rent, property taxes, and insurance have increased. According to a National Restaurant Association (NRA) study,

Chart 1.1. Foodservice Industry Growth

Year	Nominal Growth (Percentage)	Real Growth[1] (Percentage)	Total Sales ($ Billions)
1986[2]	6.6	2.8	185.3
1985	5.9	2.1	174.3
1984	8.3	4.0	164.6

[1] Percent of sales increase after adjustment for inflation.
[2] Projections.

Source: Nation's Restaurant News, (*13*).

Chart 1.2. Foodservice Growth Rate for Various Industry Segments

Segment	1984 Sales ($MM)	1984 Increase Over Previous Year (%)[1]	1985 Sales ($MM)	1985 Increase Over Previous Year (%)[1]	1986 Sales ($MM)	1986 Increase Over Previous Year (%)[1]
Full service	58.4	—	62.2	2.7	66.1	2.3
Fast–service	46.7	—	50.5	4.2	54.3	3.5
Institutional	21.2	—	21.8	1.1	22.4	−1.1
Bars/taverns	8.2	—	8.5	−0.6	8.8	−1.0
Commercial cafeterias	3.3	—	3.5	1.8	3.7	2.0
Social caterers	1.3	—	1.4	3.0	1.5	2.1
Ice cream stands	1.4	—	1.5	3.6	1.6	3.2
Total	174.3	—	185.6	2.7	197.5	2.4

[1] Percentage figures are adjusted for inflation.

Source: Nation's Restaurant News, (*24*).

"Wholesale prices, which gained only 1.6 percent in 1986 [are expected] to rise 3.4 percent in 1987. Labor costs are slated to gain 3.6 percent in 1987, up from 3.4 percent in 1986. But menu prices will advance only 4 percent, unchanged from 1986" (*24*).

In many foodservice categories menu prices have risen as foodservice operators have passed along their higher costs to guests. How-

Chart 1.3. Foodservice Projected Growth Rate for 1987 By Region	
Region	**Growth Rate (Percent)**
Rocky Mountain	8.2
South Atlantic	7.6
New England	7.2
West South Central	7.2
Pacific	6.9
East South Central	6.8
West North Central	6.0
East North Central	5.9
Middle Atlantic	5.7

Source: Nation's Restaurant News, (*24*).

ever, as competition increases, many operators are reluctant to raise prices during times which they perceive to be price sensitive. "There is a price-sensitive consumer out there. The companies that have gone the lightest on price increases are the ones that have done the best on customer counts" (*9*). Some believe that the lack of price flexibility is responsible for the current pressure on industry profit margins.

Two industry analysts credit the following factors for sluggish growth in the foodservice industry today and perhaps in the future (*15*):

- *Consumer retrenchment.* Eating out is one of the first areas to be affected by a change in consumers' disposable income. The growth in personal income has moderated in general and, combined with high debt loads and a low savings rate, has inclined consumers to eat out less.

- *Diversion of purchasing power.* Sales of hard goods have been strong and these purchases leave consumers with less money to spend on dining out.

- *Higher relative prices.* Studies of increases in prices of the grocery industry versus the foodservice industry indicate that consumers are sensitive to the relationship between the cost of food prepared at home and restaurant prices.

- *Increased level of competition.* Restaurant operators are faced with increasing competition for the consumers' away-from-home food dollars from non-traditional food outlets (convenience stores, deli counters and salad bars in supermarkets, and food outlets in department stores).

The International Foodservice Manufacturers Association (IFMA) commissioned a study which predicts continued slow growth for the foodservice industry in 1987 (23). The study shows that the deflated annual growth rate for the industry (inflation-adjusted) will slow to 1.6 percent in 1987, down from 2 percent in 1986. Most of the recent industry growth will continue to take place in an ever-shrinking segment of the market. In 1986, "The 100 largest restaurant companies increased sales by 4.7 billion dollars. But three companies—McDonald's, Pillsbury, and PepsiCo—accounted for 2.2 billion dollars of that growth" (23).

When faced with rising operating costs, the question of how a restaurant can increase the value-to-price benefit to guests without cutting into profits becomes an important consideration. One answer is better service.

Industry growth has slowed to 2 percent or less annually, yet the growing number of public companies continues to promise shareholders 10 to 15 percent compounded sales and profits each year. This growth is going to come at the expense of small- and medium-size organizations. The competition for consumers' eating-out dollars will only become more fierce. The days of simply putting more restaurants on the streets to increase sales are coming to an end and restaurateurs are looking for new and better ways to hold on to the customers they already have. Improved, caring service will be one of their key tools as they strive to develop guest loyalty.

Service Trends

Before looking at restaurant service today and where it is headed, it is important to understand how service has evolved. Historically, service has been thought of as a menial occupation. Even the word "service" conjures up visions of master-servant relationships of the past. For the most part, servants throughout history have been unskilled labor, humbly carrying out their duties according to custom and orders, with little hope of advancement.

In the post-war era of Europe, the image of restaurant service changed. Service became a respected profession requiring long training periods. In fact, today's decline in service is often attributed to the aging (and retirement) of the accomplished and disciplined group of individuals trained in post-war Europe. For these people, service was more than just a way to earn a living. It was a gratifying way of earning a good living—an avenue to professional satisfaction, achievement, and respect. This philosophy still exists in some areas of Europe and, as a result, many fine restaurants in the United States seek out European-trained personnel.

The industrialization of service is attributed to the rapid growth of the fast-service industry. The industry, which began in 1955, has grown to a 51.2 billion dollar a year entity. As fast-service operations became more prominent, quality service became linked to efficiency and speed. This link was strengthened when the industry applied the concepts of mass production and job specialization to their operations. The division of labor in fast-service establishments in which one worker prepares the food, another puts on the toppings, a third wraps the product, and so on, resulted in a highly efficient service system; one developed to ensure both speed and quality assurance. Because such service was combined with popular specialized foods, moderate prices, and cheerful and courteous point-of-sale service personnel, it satisfied the "in-a-hurry" society of the post World War II era and became the fastest growing foodservice system in the world. The "less is more" principle of the fast-service industry and budget motels worked well. It was designed to reduce the number of interactions among personnel and guests, thereby reducing costs and the opportunity for human error by placing more of the service responsibility on the guest.

However, with the loss of human interaction, there was a diminished opportunity for those vital guest-making relationships that come from courtesy, recognition, and bonding. Hospitality is one product that cannot be provided to guests by technological advances. Rather than eliminate the need for service, technological advances have added to consumers' desire for it. Service has become an important part of business and is increasingly important to consumers. The author of *Megatrends*, John Naisbitt, writes of a concept of a high-tech/high-touch society which is an accurate description of the importance of personal service in a technologically advanced economy. The more consumers are forced to deal with automated and self-service, the higher value they place on personalized service.

Much of the demand for caring service in today's economy is also based on increased discretionary purchasing power. As Karl Albrecht and Ron Zemke state in *Service America: Doing Business in a New Economy*, "As wealth increases in a population, discretionary purchasing power is created. This gives rise to a consumer-service industry able to enjoy economies of scale while accommodating a growing consumer demand for discretionary services. The demand for travel has promoted growth in airline, [restaurant, travel agency, credit card], hotel, and auto-rental companies. The demand for dining out . . . both fancy and fast has led to a highly variegated restaurant industry"(5).

Managing a business in the service economy is neither easy nor inexpensive. In the words of Theodore Levitt, author of *The Marketing Imagination,* "Efficiency in service can require as much investment in plant, equipment, and promotion as has been historically associated with efficiency in manufacturing. It can require as much planning, organization, training, controls, and capital as produced the original car [the original product] at the outset. It requires, in short, a different way of thinking about what service is, what it can be made to be, and how it must be financed" (2).

What does all this have to do with serving food? The answer is simple. Foodservice in today's economy cannot succeed by trial and error; it must be systematically designed, developed, and delivered (5). Service in all its components must be managed to meet guests' ever-changing needs and create profits for the foodservice industry.

Guests' Service Needs and Expectations

Over 40 percent of the American food dollar is spent on eating out (26). The average individual eats out about 3.7 times per week. Determining the service expectations of these guests and meeting their needs are major concerns of the industry today.

The *1985/86 Gallup Annual Report on Eating Out* revealed some interesting demographics as shown in Chart 1.4. Thirty-seven percent of adults ate one or more meals away from home on any given day in the previous year.

More young adults, age 18–24, are eating out than in past years. Consumers in this age group make up a large part of the dining-out market. However, while younger singles are an important part of the market, "There appears to be a trend toward singles under 50 years of age eating out less often, particularly the affluent, young singles" (27). The report goes on to explain that in 1979, 67 percent of young singles with incomes of $20,000 a year or more ate out on any given day. In 1985, that number dropped to 55 percent. These statistics do

Chart 1.4. Demographic Trends in Eating Out 1978-1985

| | Ate Out Yesterday* | | | | Change in |
	1978 %	1982 %	1984 %	1985 %	% pts. 1978-85
Total	34	35	37	37	+3
Sex					
Male	40	40	41	41	+1
Female	29	30	33	33	+4
Race					
White	35	36	38	37	+2
Nonwhite	27	29	31	33	+6
Age					
18-24 Years	43	45	49	48	+5
25-34 Years	40	39	42	40	0
35-49 Years	35	37	38	39	+4
50-64 Years	28	31	32	32	+4
65 Years or Older	19	22	22	22	+3
Education					
College Graduate	44	44	47	45	+1
High School Graduate	35	36	38	38	+3
Annual Household Income					
$20,000- and Over	44	42	44	44	0
$15,000-$19,999	36	33	36	36	0
Under $15,000	28	29	28	28	0
Women's Employment Status					
Full-Time	35	40	42	42	+7
Part-Time	33	32	39	39	+6
Not Employed	22	22	23	23	+1
Number of People in Household					
One	37	33	35	36	-1
Two	34	34	35	34	0
Three or Four	34	37	39	39	+5
Five or More	32	35	36	36	+4
Region					
East	32	34	35	36	+4
Midwest	34	35	37	37	+3
South	35	35	36	37	+2
West	37	36	39	38	+1

* Yesterday refers to the day before the persons were surveyed.

Source: 1985-1986 Gallup Annual Report on Eating Out as Reported in Nation's Restaurant News, (20).

not support the much touted significance of the "yuppies" (young upwardly-mobile professionals) and their impact on restaurant growth. "It is not yuppies or other baby boomers who spend the most money on food away from home—it's middle age households" (6).

The Gallup report also found that, "Additional segments of the population for which substantial increases occurred from 1978 to 1985 include nonwhites, those living in households of three or more people, and residents of the East Central section of the country, which is comprised of the states of Ohio, Michigan, Indiana, and Illinois" (27).

Chart 1.5 shows the percentages of consumers in various geographic areas who patronize different types of restaurants.

Today's restaurant guests distinguish among these restaurants to satisfy a variety of needs. These needs can be classified in five basic categories:

- *Hunger Driven.* Convenience is these guests' priority, so this need is most easily satisfied at a convenient, fast-service facility.

- *Work Avoidance.* Guests seek to avoid the work involved in shopping, food preparation, and cleaning-up. They seek a family restaurant, such as a coffee shop, or avail themselves of the growing number of home-delivered food services.

- *Socially Driven.* Guests seek friendly "Meeting, eating, and drinking places." These usually include cocktail/action lounges or casual restaurants.

- *Experience Driven.* An entertainment-type operation, such as a bistro or one-of-a-kind establishment, is used to meet these guests'

Chart 1.5. Percentages of Consumers in Various Geographic Areas Who Patronize Different Types of Restaurants

Region	Total Eating Out Population	Type of Restaurant			
		Family Type	Fast Food	Cafeteria	Adult Oriented
	%	%	%	%	%
East	25	25	24	28	28
Midwest	26	26	26	24	23
South	30	29	31	34	23
West	19	20	19	14	26

Source: 1985–1986 Gallup Annual Report on Eating Out, (27).

needs through a unique food and beverage experience. These facilities are entrepreneurial in style and have a range of prices.

- *Investment Driven.* Guests also need a place to conduct business or engage in a "courtship" for some future investment benefit. These restaurants often feature prestige and include hotel facilities, fine-dining establishments, and private clubs.

As one proceeds down the guests' needs list from top to bottom, the need for speedy service and self-help decrease, while personalized service increases.

A Gallup report found that certain customer demographics were more likely to be associated with specific types of facilities (*27*):

- *Family-type restaurants.* Guests are most likely to be: Caucasian; 50 years of age and older; married; women not working outside the home; and those in two-person households.

- *Fast-service restaurants.* Guests are most likely to be: men; non-Caucasians; 18–34 years of age; high school graduates; those with incomes under $30,000; and those in households of three or more people.

- *Cafeterias.* Guests are most likely to be: women, especially those employed full-time; non-Caucasians; 18–24 years of age; and not married.

- *Adult-oriented restaurants.* Guests are most likely to be: men; Caucasians; 35–49 years of age; upper socio-economic groups, namely college graduates or those with incomes of $30,000 and over; women working full-time; and those living in households of one or two people.

The report also profiles typical adult guests at each meal:

- Breakfast guests are most likely to be: male; 35–49 years old; have an income of $30,000 or more; or be women working full-time.

- Lunch guests are most likely to be: 25–49 years old; have an income of $20,000 and over; or be women working full-time.

- Dinner guests are most likely to be: Caucasian; and have an income of $30,000 and over.

Chart 1.6 shows the percentages of people who eat out at various meals.

Chart 1.6. Percentages of People Who Eat Out at Various Meals

	Total Eating Out Population %	Meal Eaten Out		
		Breakfast %	Lunch %	Dinner %
Sex				
Male	53	65	52	54
Female	47	35	48	46
Race				
White	88	90	87	91
Non-white	12	10	13	9
Age				
18-24 years	21	16	21	20
25-34 years	26	26	27	25
35-49 years	26	30	27	26
50-64 years	18	19	17	19
65 years and older	9	9	8	10
Education				
College graduate	24	25	26	24
High school graduate	61	58	61	61
Less than high school graduate	15	17	13	15
Annual Household Income				
$30,000 and over	41	45	43	43
$20,000-$29,999	24	23	25	22
$15,000-$19,999	12	12	11	12
Under $15,000	23	20	21	23
Marital Status				
Married	58	56	56	60
Not married	42	44	44	40
Women's Employment Status				
Full-time	50	57	55	47
Part-time	17	14	16	18
Not employed	33	29	29	35
Number of People in Household				
One	16	18	16	16
Two	30	30	29	32
Three or four	40	38	41	39
Five or more	14	14	14	13
Region				
East	25	25	25	25

Chart 1.6. Percentages of People Who Eat Out at Various Meals (continued)

	Total Eating Out Population %	Meal Eaten Out		
		Breakfast %	Lunch %	Dinner %
Midwest	26	25	24	27
South	30	31	31	28
West	19	19	20	20

Source: 1985-1986 Gallup Annual Report on Eating Out, (27).

It is believed that in the future, older consumers will have an increasing impact on the foodservice industry. According to the United States Census Bureau, the median age in 1970 was 28; in the year 2000, it will have risen to 36. The number of people over 55 years of age is expected to total over 59 million by the turn of the century (10).

An industry article predicts that the maturing baby boom generation will impact on foodservice. "Healthier foods, low in fat and sodium, less red meat, more chicken and fish, less alcohol, more upscale and diverse menus—these are what the roughly 69 million men and women born between 1946 and 1962 say they want today. Further projections indicate that as they age, they'll be more willing and able to afford eating out; they are more affluent, educated, and service oriented than any generation that's come before" (8).

New Lifestyles ... New Needs, New Wants

The Changing Role of Women

An important lifestyle change that has affected the foodservice industry is the increase of women in the work force. In the United States today, over 50 percent of adult women are employed or are looking for employment. These women have more money and less time to spend it. They are in search of convenient, easy ways to feed themselves and their families.

The number of women who eat away from home has increased significantly since 1978. Women, especially those employed outside the home, were responsible for most of the increase in the number of people dining out. "The incidence of eating out among women employed full-time jumped seven percentage points, while a six-point gain occurred among women employed on a part-time basis. Overall, among all women, the incidence of eating out over the seven year period [of the study] increased by four percentage points, while only a one-point increase can be observed among men" (27).

The Traditional Male Role Also Changes

Traditionally, men have worked full-time and continue to do so, but now they also juggle their work with increased involvement in child care, shopping for food, home activities, and health- and fitness-related activities. They are feeling the squeeze on their leisure time. Their high stress levels and complicated lifestyles have increased the demand for convenience and time savings in foodservice throughout the country.

Changing Preferences

Guests' tastes have become more sophisticated. To them, eating out can be a convenience or an adventure. The contemporary public is excited about and interested in food, and wants choices. For example, ethnic foods are growing in popularity. One survey found that 28 percent of consumers give more of their business to an ethnic restaurant than to any American-style restaurant (16).

The same survey found that 28 percent of consumers name an ethnic outlet as their favorite dining establishment and 14 percent of those who do so frequent their favorite spot more than once a week. Chart 1.7 shows consumer preferences for favorite types of restaurants; while Chart 1.8 shows the types of foods consumers prefer to order.

The Concern With Nutrition

Nutrition is a major concern of many of today's diners and is affecting both dining-out and eating-at-home decisions (27). One survey indicated that 40 percent of adult consumers have altered their menu choices at restaurants to reflect better nutrition; 60 percent have adjusted their eating habits at home because of health and nutrition concerns. Among those who have changed their menu choices in restaurants (22):

- 26 percent say they eat more vegetables.

- 23 percent have reduced salt intake.

- 22 percent have cut back on sugar.

- 21 percent order more seafood dishes.

Chart 1.7. Consumer Preferences for Favorite Types of Restaurants

	Total	Sex		Age			Income			Region			
		M	F	21-34	35-54	55 & older	Under $25,000	$25,000-$34,999	$35,000 or more	Northeast	South	Midwest	West
American	68%	64%	70%	60%	65%	83%	73%	73%	59%	65%	70%	72%	62%
Chinese	7	5	8	8	8	3	7	6	8	7	10	6	5
Italian	6	8	5	9	6	4	5	8	7	11	4	4	3
Mexican	6	5	6	9	6	*	7	6	6	3	3	7	12
French	3	3	4	3	5	2	1	1	8	5	2	1	6
Japanese	2	3	1	4	1	1	2	1	3	1	2	1	5
Greek	2	3	1	1	2	2	1	*	2	1	2	2	1
Other	2	3	3	3	3	2	2	3	4	4	3	2	2

* No responses, or too few to be statistically significant.

Source: Nation's Restaurant News, (16).

Chart 1.8. Types of Foods Consumers Prefer to Order

	% of All Meals	Sex		Age			Income			Region			
		M	F	21-34	35-54	55 & older	Under $25,000	$25,000-$34,999	$35,000 or more	North-east	South	Mid-west	West
American	74%	73%	75%	69%	74%	81%	72%	78%	71%	74%	79%	75%	67%
Italian	9	11	8	11	9	7	10	8	11	10	7	9	10
Chinese	7	7	7	7	8	6	7	5	9	7	7	6	9
Mexican	4	4	4	6	3	3	4	4	4	2	4	4	7
French	1	*	1	1	1	*	1	*	1	1	*	1	1
Japanese	1	*	1	1	*	*	1	*	1	1	*	*	1
Other	1	1	1	2	1	1	1	1	2	2	1	1	1

* Less than 0.5%

Source: Nation's Restaurant News, (16).

- 20 percent try to consume less fat.

- 18 percent order more salads.

- 17 percent order less meat.

- 15 percent attempt to avoid fried foods.

Chart 1.9 shows how consumer attitudes about healthier foods are segmented (21).

New At-home Lifestyle

Increased pressures in daily life have prompted more consumers to spend more time at home as a refuge from the hectic outside world. In order to enjoy their homes, consumers are making them more comfortable and attractive. Technological advances such as microwave ovens and video systems have made staying at home a convenient way to entertain and be entertained. These changes in lifestyle have contributed to the boom in take-out and home-delivery foodservice. By 1990, it is predicted that, "Twenty-five percent of all meals eaten in the home will be purchased fully prepared, creating a tremendous new window of opportunity within the industry" (25).

Many experts believe take-out foodservice is important to the future of the industry. "Restaurants and fast-service outlets are introducing or experimenting with take-out in an effort to satisfy consumer demand for convenience, quickness, and variety in meals, [and restaurateurs] are discovering that take-out offers the potential for increased volume, profitability, and utilization of assets" (11).

Chart 1.9. Consumer Attitudes Toward Healthier Foods

| Consumer Group | % of Adult Population | % of Reported Occasions | | | |
		Total	Fast Food	Moderately Priced	Fine Dining
Traditional	37%	43%	46%	39%	32%
Weight Conscious	28	25	23	26	31
Health Conscious	19	17	16	16	26
Uncommitted	12	12	12	14	8
Not in a Group	4	3	3	5	3

Source: Nation's Restaurant News, (21).

The statistics are overwhelming. Consumers are spending about 24–30 billion dollars on take-out foods (*11*). Consumer Reports on Eating-Out Share Trends (CREST), a survey of restaurant trends, has found that 39.5 percent of all guest traffic in the year ending May 31, 1985, consisted of take-out business (*25*). Of those consumers, 60 percent ate the take-out food at home; 17 percent ate in "other" places; 13 percent ate in their cars; and 10 percent ate at work. "The most frequent take-out consumers include women, those aged 18–34, singles, families with teenagers, households where the female head is employed, and households with incomes from $20,000 to $50,000" (*25*). Chart 1.10 shows the types of foods being purchased by take-out consumers (*14*). With many of the same consumers and for many of the same reasons, the home-delivery foodservice market is growing as well.

The maturing of America is expected to have far-reaching effects on consumers' needs and wants. A Bureau of Labor survey has found that older consumers tend to eat more fresh fruits and vegetables and drink less alcohol. Interestingly enough, older consumers tend to buy less food away from home. "Economists predict that the effect of an aging population on spending for food away from home will be a drop of almost 4 percent. However, rising incomes [in the next few decades]

Chart 1.10. Take-Out Foods Preferred by Customers[1]

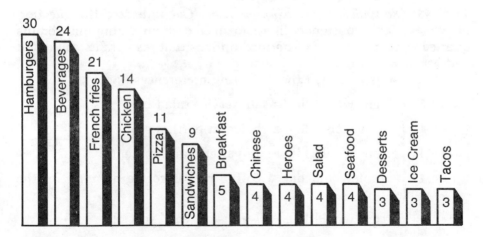

[1] Figures are expressed as percentages.

Source: Nation's Restaurant News, (*14*).

will offset the age factor, boosting money spent in restaurants a massive 66.8 percent" (*19*). Restaurant features that tend to appeal to older guests include lighter, healthier foods, more comfortable seating, smaller portions, and early breakfast and dinner service.

Attitudes and Expectations Regarding Service

These demographic shifts and lifestyle changes have prompted new attitudes and expectations among foodservice guests. Today's guests expect more when they dine out. The "I deserve more" philosophy prevails in many segments of society. In light of this growing consumer attitude, service has become a crucial factor in ensuring a restaurant's success. In one survey, restaurant guests reported that, "No matter how good the food was, bad service made the experience incomplete. A waiter or waitress who can pick up the guest's mood and adapt accordingly, will increase the quality of the evening" (*7*). Another study looked at the psychographics (psychological profiles of market segments) of four consumer groups and its results are shown in Chart 1.11.

What Guests Like and Don't Like About Eating Out

The *1985/86 Gallup Annual Report on Eating Out* addressed the question of what today's consumers like and dislike about eating out. Adults queried were given a list of defined options that restaurants could add and asked which they would choose.

The results indicated the following preferences (*27*):

- 57 percent would like a self-service salad bar.

- 47 percent would like a choice in portion size.

- 44 percent would like more variety on the menu.

- 42 percent would like a coffee pot or coffee decanter on the table.

- 37 percent would like "all-you-can-eat" specials.

- 30 percent would like a complimentary service such as a relish tray, glass of wine, or after-dinner beverage.

- 30 percent would like a self-service soup bar.

Chart 1.11. Psychographics of Four Consumer Groups

Group 1: Consumers Who Like New and Different Experiences, Quiet and Attractive Restaurants.

- I prefer quiet, attractive restaurants.
- I frequently try new items on the menu.
- I prefer to order seafood when I eat out.
- I like trying new restaurants.
- I like to order ethnic foods when I eat out.
- I like to order food out that I don't get or prepare at home.

Most Commonly Are:	Less Commonly Are:
Women (40%)	Men (26%)
Caucasians (34%)	Non-caucasians (27%)
25-29 years of age (38%)	65 years of age or older (22%)
College graduates (50%)	Non-High School Graduates (19%)
Earners $30,000 or more yearly (45%)	Earners under $15,000 yearly (24%)
Working women (44%)	Non-working women (36%)
Westerners (40%)	Southerners (28%)
People who eat out four or more times per week (45%)	People who do not eat out in an average week (25%)

Group 2: Meat Lovers.

- I like to eat steak or beef dishes when I eat out.
- A main meal is not complete without beef.

Most Commonly Are:	Less Commonly Are:
Men (41%)	Women (26%)
18-24 years of age (43%)	25-34 years of age (29%)
High school graduates (37%)	College graduates (23%)
Earners under $15,000 yearly (39%)	Earners $30,000 or more yearly (27%)
Singles 18-50 years of age (37%)	Singles 50 years of age or older (33%)
Southerners (38%)	Easterners (28%)
Midwesterners (37%)	Westerners (28%)
People who eat out at least once in an average week (38%)	People who don't eat out in an average week (28%)

Chart 1.11. Psychographics of Four Consumer Groups (continued)

Group 3: Customers Who Like Quick Service and Inexpensive Meals.
- I prefer fast-service or casual restaurants.
- I prefer eating at restaurants with which I am familiar.
- I would prefer to eat several less expensive meals than one meal at an expensive place.
- Being able to get my food quickly is important to me when I eat out.

Most Commonly Are:	Less Commonly Are:
Men (36%)	Women (31%)
Non-caucasians (37%)	Caucasians (33%)
18-24 years of age (43%)	50-64 years of age (30%)
Residents in households with three or more people (38%)	Residents in households with one or two people (28%)
Non-high school graduates (42%)	College graduates (22%)
Singles 18-50 years of age (35%)	Singles 50 years of age or older (29%)
Midwesterners (38%)	Easterners (28%)
Southerners (38%)	Westerners (28%)

Group 4: Food and Restaurant Lovers.
- If I could afford it, I would eat all of my meals out.
- I like restaurants that serve large portions.
- I like restaurants that offer entertainment.
- I usually eat fast.
- My favorite part of the meal is dessert.
- I usually eat more food when I eat out than when I eat at home.

Most Commonly Are:	Less Commonly Are:
Men (37%)	Women (30%)
Non-caucasians (41%)	Caucasians (32%)
18-24 years of age (54%)	65 years of age or older (17%)
Singles (42%)	Married adults (29%)
Earners between $20,000 and $29,000 yearly (39%)	Earners $30,000 or more yearly (27%)
Singles 18-50 years of age	Singles 50 years of age or older (21%)

Source: Nation's Restaurant News, (*18*).

Features that were chosen by a lower percentage of consumers (14–16 percent) included:

- Each menu item offered separately.
- Dieter's specials.
- Food items on display before you buy them.
- A wider selection of wines.

The same survey asked consumers what circumstances in a restaurant would cause them not to return.

- 83 percent said poor service.
- 64 percent expressed a dislike for loud music.
- 61 percent mentioned slow service.
- 47 percent said they dislike restaurants where it is too dark to properly see the menu or the food.
- 46 percent dislike tables that are too close.
- 36 percent said the lack of a non-smoking section.

Other factors guests dislike include the following:

- A lack of sanitation in any area of the facility.
- Poor table locations, perhaps near service areas or other passages.
- Tables that are too small or are too close to one another (unless they are purposely so because of a particular facility's ambiance).
- Uncomfortable chairs.
- Environments that are too hot, cold, or drafty.
- Restrooms that are too small, dirty, or poorly supplied.

Service Speed Grows in Importance

The number of guests who would not return to a restaurant where they received slow service has risen 8 percent since 1982. In general, guests are becoming less tolerant of annoyances in restaurants. Since 1982, each of the annoyances mentioned in the survey would cause more consumers (2–14 percent more) not to return to a restaurant today.

Assessing guests' preferences and complaints is especially critical to restaurant service because guests do not usually complain when they are dissatisfied. According to the *1985/86 Gallup Annual Report on Eating Out* (*27*), when adults across the country were asked what action they would take if they were dissatisfied with the food or service in a restaurant, the replies varied for fine-dining restaurants, family-style restaurants, and fast-service restaurants. Many of those surveyed replied that they would avoid a restaurant in the future or tell their friends about the bad experience, rather than complain to a server or manager. "Today's public is the most educated dining public in the history of this country. They're more critical, less compassionate, and have many options about where to dine out . . . most of them are not going to give you a second chance if you fail" (*12*).

2
Attracting and Keeping Customers

What Makes the Difference?

During meal periods, walk down any street that has a few restaurants on it. Invariably, some establishments will have every table occupied, while others will have few, if any, guests. Attracting guests is a function of identifying a target market and both promising and delivering what it wants in the way of menu, tastes, services, ambiance, and value-to-price offerings.

Using effective advertising and promotional techniques (such as discounting and special events) is the most common way to attract new guests. However, acquiring new guests is really only half the battle to build demand. The other half is retaining them. Keeping patrons satisfied and coming back is the most cost-effective way to build a loyal guest following. This is called *internal marketing.* It is the function of what is often called "operations." Industry research bears this out. "It is five times more expensive to acquire a new customer than to keep an old one" (4).

The foodservice business is one where there is no division between operations and marketing. They cannot be separated. It requires a relentless commitment by management and crew to view guest satisfaction as the organizational purpose or reason for being. To this end, it is what is done to retain the loyalty of guests while they are inside the restaurant that is most important. The loyalty of guests is not built by mass communication, but by individual persuasion one guest at a time. This takes place inside the restaurant.

Today, in most areas of the country, consumers can purchase, take-out, or have delivered gourmet and ethnic foods from different types of establishments. Thus, a restaurant needs to add a value greater than quality food to compete. Consumers are tired of waiting for assistance, being treated impersonally, and receiving mediocre service in many areas of day-to-day life—from service stations to doctors' offices. Foodservice is one area where guests have many alternatives. They expect quality service and if they don't get it, they can almost always find another establishment in the vicinity that will provide it. Restaurateurs can attract a clientele by offering guests the type of service they desire.

Guest restaurant preferences arise from the host of sociological and psychological factors relating to food and service that were discussed in Chapter 1. Creating a successful restaurant is a difficult task. To achieve the highest standards, managers monitor technical details, while focusing on their guests' satisfaction. They must pay attention to food quality and presentation. Just keeping hot food hot and cold food cold is a time-consuming task in a restaurant.

Food means different things to different people. Food and beverage tastes are highly personal and eating patterns stem from a person's upbringing and environment. "In addition to the foods people have available, food habits depend on a combination of psychological, [sociological], and biochemical factors. [Generally] people eat what [is familiar and tastes good to them, and sometimes what] they think is good for them. Food patterns are based on food lore and in part (at least in modern, technologically-developed countries) on commercial advertising and sound knowledge of nutritional needs" (1). Food choices are affected by the foods available and a guest's cultural background, area of residence, family composition, values (such as a need for status or the desire to be physically fit), and available budget.

These factors are at work whether guests are conscious of them or not. The aroma of certain foods can trigger memories (both pleasant and unpleasant); different types of foods are associated with special occasions (birthday cakes and birthdays or champagne as a way to celebrate); and other foods have taken on meanings of comfort or love because of past experiences with them (chocolate as a reward or chicken soup for healing). A restaurant needs to evoke positive food associations from its guests, and avoid the negative. To do this, managers must focus on the guests' tastes, and not their own.

Guests must also feel positive about food presentation and service. The appeal of food depends on its aroma, color, texture, shape, and taste. Service must be provided in a manner consistent with or exceeding a guest's expectations. If it is not, guests will be disappointed and not return to the restaurant. Depending on their background and values, some guests will feel comfortable with a particular type of restaurant service; while others will be ill at ease with it. A guest who enters a restaurant expecting family-style service and finds formal, fine-dining service will be dissatisfied. Or, very formal service in a family-style establishment will make some patrons uncomfortable. The secret to attracting a large appropriate following is to design service strategies that will appeal to a restaurant's target group.

Basic requirements for attracting and keeping restaurant guests include:

- *The right position (image).* Restaurants need to convey what it is they offer to potential guests. The right combination of facility design, menu, food, service, and staff is required to build an appealing image.

- *Quality.* Guests expect quality that is appropriate to the type of restaurant, the type of food served, and the prices charged. The term quality is ambiguous—it has various interpretations and arouses different expectations. Commonly, it is associated with the taste of the food and beverages. Guests do not expect to find pre-prepared frozen sundaes in gourmet ice cream specialty shops, but might accept these items in fast-service establishments. Guests do not expect to see fresh flowers in diners (although some do have them), but would be surprised if they were not to be found in fine-dining facilities. Guests in all restaurants expect food to be safe, sanitary, well-prepared, and tasty.

- *Service.* Guests perceive more caring service than expected as an *added value;* while unfeeling, poorer quality service than expected makes them feel cheated and influences them not to return.

Patrons of any type of restaurant want to be waited on to the appropriate degree (even in a self-service restaurant), be served within a reasonable period, receive fair value for their money, and be treated with care and respect.

- *An appropriate menu.* Guests expect a menu to fit the type of restaurant—a limited menu in a fast-service outlet, a full, but simple menu in a family restaurant, and a creative gourmet menu in a fine-dining establishment. They appreciate menu copy that is accurate and easy to understand; adequate food portions (neither too overwhelming nor skimpy); and prices that are in line with what's offered. Using menu specials adds interest and excitement to the menu and gives guests the impression of added value. As a rule, a menu should be creative, but not too trendy. Trendy menus have limited appeal (usually to higher income, experience-oriented diners) and are destined to be short-lived. Of course, menus should have an appealing design and always be presented to guests in top condition.

- *Presentation.* Like quality, presentation must also be appropriate to the type of restaurant, the type of food being served, and the prices charged. When guests are paying fine-dining prices, they expect food to be presented creatively with a special touch. Experts agree that guests can be influenced to purchase an item if it is packaged to exceed their expectations (2). This idea is especially true for food presentation because taste, touch, sight, smell, and hearing are all integral parts of the dining-out experience. To exceed expectations, food must appeal to all the senses. This can be achieved by being creative with the colors, textures, and shapes of the food, using unique serviceware and garnishes, and providing the appropriate music to complete the dining experience. Guests appreciate when steaks sizzle on platters; freshly baked crusty bread steams on a wooden board; red, juicy strawberries are served in crystal goblets; or a dip is served in a colorful, hollowed-out vegetable.

Guests' service requirements are situational. The same guests will have different needs at different times. For example, mothers who work outside the home may require quick noontime meals, take-out food for family dinners, and entertaining evenings out with family or friends all in the same week.

Restaurants are increasingly aware of this and similar phenomena and are engaging in what has been named "niche marketing" or positioning to meet their guests' multiple needs (20). The "Challenge is the consumer's maddening mix of identities" (20). Foodservice companies serve guests from a variety of demographic groups. Their concepts must serve a differentiated population without fragmenting the image to such an extent that they lose their reason for being. Managers face many opportunities. "Today, the need is for take-out; tomorrow, [catering or home or office] delivery; next week, a special occasion celebration. This chameleon customer can, if not properly identified, create confusion . . . Niche marketing is oriented first to people; second to product; third to place; and finally, to occasion" (20). Attracting guests is based on knowing what a particular market niche of consumers seeks.

Statistics show that 37 percent of adults in this country eat one or more meals away from home daily. These guests are from all walks of life and represent every segment of the population. Individual restaurants have different potential guests based on their location, pricing, type of menu, and service style. Savvy restaurateurs take into account the trading area, its people, and the competition. They use both quantitative and qualitative market research to ascertain the demographics and preferences of potential customers—how and where guests earn a living, how often they eat out, why they eat out, what they order, and what atmosphere and types of service they prefer.

Quantitative market research yields data that tell the number, types, and habits of consumers. Most companies conduct some form of their own quantitative research. In addition, there are various research organizations and trade publications specializing in the foodservice field (see the Appendix for a listing) that provide numerical data on how many consumers eat out, how often, what meals they eat out most frequently, and what products they select.

Accurate quantitative market data are needed for managerial decision-making. For example, this data can help managers anticipate what menu to serve, know when to expect peak guest hours, and schedule employees accordingly. The data may indicate that a restaurant should emphasize quick breakfast service because the research shows that an increasing number of guests are attracted to facilities that serve them a convenient breakfast before they go to work. Using quantitative market research, management can monitor traffic trends and adjust their service design. If a rush of guests at breakfast makes it difficult for employees to handle their requests for coffee refills, management might decide to have servers place a thermal carafe of coffee on each table.

Qualitative market research provides management with an inside look at the attitudes, opinions, and expectations of guests. It reveals what qualities of service they value. Properly assessing the subjective opinions of guests is critical. For instance, how do guests feel when servers introduce themselves by name before presenting them with menus? This is practiced successfully by some establishments and abhorred by others. Restaurateurs need to assess their guests' preferences before considering this service approach.

To be useful, market research must be current and correctly interpreted. Although guests want change, management must distinguish between fads and trends. Fads come and go quickly. What is in one year may be off-base the next.

Consumer desires change slowly, producing much conflict during transitional periods. For example, despite guests' increased interest in well-being and lighter eating, many are also opting for rich desserts. Ice cream consumption in restaurants reached an all-time high last year. Serving diners a light, broiled fish entrée and then encouraging them to order a sumptuous dessert may seem contradictory. However, this combination of light and rich eating is exactly what many of today's guests want. Restaurant operators who use the latest market research to keep abreast of guests' changing preferences have the advantage of being prepared to meet the challenge of providing more and better service. To gain this information, restaurateurs rely on the following tools:

- *Menu Sales Mix Histories.* Analyzing performances of past menu mixes reveals a great deal about a restaurant's guests and their changing tastes. Which menu offerings were well received and which were not? Which hours of the day, days of the week, and times of the year offer peak crowds? At what times is business especially slow?

- *Guest Surveys.* One of the best ways to learn more about guests is to ask for their input. This can be done on an informal, one-to-one basis as guests dine or as they leave the restaurant. It can also be done in a more formal manner using guest comment cards left on the table, exit intercepts, or a follow-up survey mailed to guests. Without getting feedback from the guest, a restaurant operator might not realize that diners are annoyed by the background music in the restaurant, find the menu hard to read, or feel they are being rushed by a particular server. Some facilities conduct quarterly guest audits or opinion surveys.

- *Consumer Focus Groups.* Consumer focus groups, a useful form of qualitative research developed by advertising researchers, are used by many businesses to explore consumer needs. Restaurant operators can use this method by inviting a typical cross-section of potential guests (typically 8 to 10 people) to a meeting in which a moderator leads a discussion about what the guests like and dislike about the restaurant, including menu, pricing, cleanliness, and the behavior and appearance of personnel. A list of key questions should be prepared in advance of the meeting and the person conducting the group should be alert to attitudes and trends which emerge during the discussion. Often, such discussions are taped, so restaurant operators can better analyze the opinions expressed.

- *Industry Resources.* A variety of publications is available to help foodservice operators keep abreast of industry trends, including *Nation's Restaurant News, Quick Frozen Foods, Restaurant Business, Restaurants & Institutions, Restaurants U.S.A.,* and *Restaurant Hospitality.* Consumer food magazines also alert operators to food trends and preferences. Other sources of information include the National Restaurant Association (NRA), the International Foodservice Manufacturers Association (IFMA), the International Franchise Association (IFA), and various educational institutions with hospitality and home study programs.

After they identify their potential clientele, restaurateurs can design and deliver the products and services necessary to attract and satisfy these guests. Guests must be the basis for every management decision.

The Importance of a Marketing Strategy

Although some guests are attracted to a restaurant by chance, restaurateurs cannot rely on luck. They require a consumer-based marketing strategy to attract a clientele. A marketing strategy is a plan for attracting and satisfying guests by providing a competitive advantage. It has four basic components (*3*):

- Conducting a situation analysis to determine market opportunities. A situation analysis is the study of four social and economic elements to determine the strengths, weaknesses, opportunities, and threats to a business in a given trade area. These are:

The restaurant's history and current operating situation.

Trade area trends and traffic generators.

The competition.

Consumer demands.

- Selecting a target audience and restaurant concept with a competitive position.

- Formulating a mission statement and marketing action program that will take the business where it needs to go.

- Implementing and controlling the program.

Opportunity determination and target market selection is the result of situation analysis. They are the detective work that is required to create a restaurant concept with a competitive advantage, which is a challenge in today's saturated restaurant market place. They involve knowing the guest and measuring potential "Consumer demand (opportunity) against supply (competition) at its local site level by several different groups and by select business segments including meal period, day, eat-in/take out, etc." (20). Once the target market and its needs have been established, a competitive restaurant concept is designed. Restaurateurs decide the product-service mix, pricing, packaging, and the communication-promotion mix. (See Chapter 4 for a discussion of products, service styles, and presentation). The mission statement addresses the issue of where management wants to take the business over a given period (usually 5 years). The marketing plan spells out the actions that need to be taken to achieve the mission. The last step is to put the plan into action and monitor it day by day and week to week.

Advertising's Role

Advertising is used by restaurants to:

- Create consumer awareness.

- Provide information about a facility or product.

- Establish a market position.

- Project a desired image.

- Promote products and services.

- Help distinguish the facility from its competition.

"The typical restaurant spends 5 to 6 percent of gross sales on rent, 25 to 30 percent on labor, 30 to 38 percent on food and beverages, but only 2.2 percent on advertising" (*10*).

Restaurant advertising is based on (*10*):

- Type of product (ethnic, gourmet, fast-service, and so forth).

- Target audience (upscale, family, singles, etc.).

- Competitors (who they are and what positioning they have adopted).

- Pricing structure.

With these factors in mind, restaurant management determines its advertising strategy. Advertising is positioned with the following in mind:

- The advertising budget.

- Desired results, i.e. awareness, trial, new product introduction, retrial, etc.

- Target audience and its communicating habits.

- The message to be conveyed.

- The media to be used.

- Promotional periods.

- Competitive activities.

- Evaluation.

Newspapers, magazines, radio, television, flyers (both hand-out and direct mail), and billboards are the most frequently used restaurant advertising media.

Public Relations Functions

Public relations involves activities and techniques designed to bring about favorable attitudes and reactions to a business. Effective public relations helps create a positive public image for the facility and builds guest goodwill.

In the restaurant industry, public relations may consist of:

- *Sponsorship of or contributions to community events.* In addition to supporting popular business-funded charities, such as United Way or Meals on Wheels, restaurants also contribute money, food, other products, or their services to local charities, facilities, or sports teams.

- *Participation in local events by the facility's employees.* Encouraging employees to run in marathons sponsored by local hospitals or to serve meals at community shelters are examples of employee participation that shows that the restaurant is concerned with the community. However, these activities must not be undertaken at the expense of the employees' performance on the job.

- *Media appearances or interviews with a restaurant employee.* Sometimes, issues arise requiring a restaurant employee to appear on radio or television or be interviewed for print articles. Reporters are either seeking an opinion on an issue affecting the industry, or the restaurant itself is involved in an issue or event. Companies typically have strict policies and procedures regarding who can represent the company. These employees have, or are given, special media training so that the facility can be represented positively.

- *Newspaper and magazine articles, books, or television and radio shows that feature or mention the restaurant.* Restaurants frequently have public relations programs aimed at generating publicity in print or on electronic media. Some invite guest chefs or other celebrities to make appearances; others offer free seminars or cooking classes. A few devise stunts, such as the company that sponsored the making of the world's largest ice cream sundae. Restaurateurs need to employ professionals or use professional techniques to ensure that publicity attempts succeed.

Word-of-Mouth (WOM) Advertising

Many managers feel the frustration of limited advertising and public relations budgets. They witness the results of the powerful campaigns of some of the fast-service chains. However, the persuasive power of advertising is not limited to fast-service companies; other restaurants drive their messages home powerfully through the media.

Unfortunately, too many restaurateurs overlook their most effective and efficient promotional medium, that of word-of-mouth (WOM). In fact, a recent Gallup survey revealed that in 44 percent of cases when consumers try a new restaurant, the reason given for the visit was "a recommendation." According to the report, word-of-mouth advertising was the leading reason for guests trying a new restaurant (24).

Why is word-of-mouth advertising so powerful? First, it is highly persuasive. As a rule, the person conveying the message to the next person has the two most important persuasion qualities—trust and respect. The message carrier has little to gain from offering the recommendation, but does take some risk—losing trust and respect if the recommendation proves to be inaccurate.

Second, word-of-mouth is influential. It usually comes from first-person experience and involves reliable information about a restaurant. In addition, it is said with conviction, which is one of the most effective tools of persuasion.

Third, word-of-mouth is directed to a highly segmented audience, the friends and associates of current guests. Consumers usually trust the experiences of family, friends, relatives, neighbors, and others of the same social class (24).

While most restaurateurs recognize that word-of-mouth is a very effective persuasive force, few appreciate that it can be managed. Word-of-mouth advertising is effective, and can be systematically implemented through WOM campaigns. But, word-of-mouth advertising does not just happen. Like any successful advertising campaign, it has to be planned with as much effort as other types of advertising.

Word-of-mouth can be a very sophisticated and planned campaign. The basic ingredient for successful word-of-mouth advertising is consistency of high-quality standards. The restaurant must unfailingly live up to its reputation so as not to disappoint guests who have come to the restaurant on someone's recommendation.

The keys to positive WOM are: 1) the exceeded expectation—the goal of every successful restaurateur and staff should be to provide a level of service that more than satisfies the guest; and 2) to provide guests with the information and language to tell others about their experience—successful word-of-mouth programs are designed to encourage guests to talk to their friends and associates.

The design for a successful WOM campaign is as follows:

- Have planned internal activities that will cause people to talk.
- Support the activities with a budget (as in any promotional campaign).
- Use service personnel as the advertising agents.
- Make the guests' WOM the medium.

- Establish that the target audience is the friends, family, and associates of the guests.

What Makes People Talk?

There are steps restaurateurs can take to ensure that people will talk about pleasant experiences at a particular restaurant (24):

- *Provide the unexpected extra.* Offer guests a tangible or intangible extra for which they do not pay. Tangibles range from a special dinner salad prepared just for them to items such as glassware, ashtrays, or mementos to take away with them. Intangibles may be personalized recognition from the management.

- *Enable people to share pioneering experiences.* Make guests feel like pioneers by offering them an opportunity to try or sample a new taste experience. Provide interesting information with the sample to give guests the background for good conversation about the experience.

- *Establish the guest as an authority.* Help guests become authorities by sharing with them food or beverage knowledge that they can pass on to others. Having this knowledge should make them want to talk to others.

- *Make consultants out of guests.* Invite guests to act as consultants by asking their opinions on menu, presentation, decor, and new concepts. Besides making guests feel special, this technique provides valuable customer research data.

- *Reveal "inside" information.* Provide guests with "inside" information, such as a forthcoming menu offering, expansion plans, the chef's "secret" recipes, or allowing them to tour the kitchen.

- *Recognize guests.* Acknowledge guests on sight and address them by name during their dining experience.

Internal Sales Promotion Techniques

Promotional techniques are activities designed to influence customers' purchasing decisions. While many experts agree that up to 75 percent of consumers have already made their purchase decision before they select the restaurant, there still exists opportunity for promoting impulse sales. As one industry expert explains it, merchandising is "Providing consumers the opportunity to increase their enjoyment of a dining experience through additional purchases" (2). The objectives of good internal promotional programs are to increase (2):

- Guest level of enjoyment (real or perceived) of the total food experience, thus increasing the frequency of visits.

- Average check through the additional sale of appetizers, desserts, and beverages.

- Party size.

- The likelihood guests will have a lasting, memorable experience that will be shared with others.

The following promotional techniques are used in the restaurant industry to increase both customer satisfaction and profits.

The Menu/Wine List

The menu is one way a restaurant communicates with its guests. Effective menus are innovative, enticing, and exciting. They are designed to capture the guest's interest and positively influence purchase decisions.

An effective menu's layout and design direct a guest's eye to the most popular and profitable offerings. Proportion, white space, contrast, graphics, color, copy, type, and descriptions come together in a complementary way and make the most of the space available. Good promotional menus can be entertaining and enhance the restaurant's desired image, but must also contain a pleasing arrangement of offerings that are printed clearly and in an organized manner.

Menu clip-ons, such as listings of "specials," are used to attract a guest's attention and merchandise products successfully. Menu clutter, which makes a menu difficult to read, must be avoided.

Appealing wine lists contain a variety of products consistent with the image of the restaurant and targeted to its clientele. Guests prefer lists to be organized and clearly written. They want product prices to be apparent.

One notable wine list at an Oregon establishment offers 1,100 different wines, but was designed to meet guests' needs. The cellar master says, "With all those choices, I've had to create a wine list that does not frustrate a customer by its very size, one that would be easy to handle. I think we now have one of the best-organized lists in the country. It's set up to discourage flipping pages because, in my experience, people will open to one page, flip back and forth and if they don't see something they want, they become discouraged" (12).

Creative promotional techniques involving menus and wine lists that have been used by some facilities include:

- Drink menus filled with graffiti created by their guests.

- T-shirt menus worn by servers poolside at a hotel.

- Wine lists on balloons which are blown up by servers at the table.

- Acrylic menus with items drawn on with magic markers.

- Menus containing caricatures of celebrated guests who frequent the establishment.

- Menus imprinted on placements or tablecloths.

- Menus written on paddles, boards, or racquets.

- Children's menus that can be made into puppets or animals.

- Use of cartoons, riddles, or humorous descriptions on the menu to amuse guests.

When creative menu and wine list techniques are used, restaurateurs must ensure that the creative aspects of these items do not overshadow the practical factors. Guests still require menus that are easy to read.

Suggestive Selling

Suggestive selling is the primary means of impacting on guests' purchasing decisions. In fact, one industry experiment showed that the average guest check can be increased by 50 percent when a server simply suggests products to guests (2).

Facilities merchandise successfully by using four suggestive selling techniques.

- *Employ persuasive people.* To use suggestive selling effectively, a restaurant must select the right type of personnel and train them in the techniques of suggestive selling.

- *Establish a merchandising climate.* Creating a friendly, hospitable environment that generates goodwill is a critical factor in increasing the dollar amount of guest checks. Personnel can accomplish this by aiming to make each guest feel like the most important person in the restaurant. Nothing is quite as uplifting to guests as entering a restaurant and being greeted by name. By making an effort to remember guests' names, giving attention to special orders, offering suggestions for favorite items, and giving guests "inside information" about the menu, servers can make guests feel catered to and special.

- *Maintain enthusiasm.* Restaurants need to ensure that employees sustain enthusiasm by establishing new product, promotion, and incentive programs. Managers need to provide a means for employees to grow with their jobs.

- *Use the AIDA system.* It has four components—attention, interest, desire, and action (*2*):

  Attention for products is generated by: a service person's enthusiastic approach; innovative packaging; and attention-getting devices, such as unusual menus, flaming foods, or sizzler platters.

  Servers create *interest* in products when they ask leading questions ("Have you ever tasted ...?") or make recommendations ("They're serving my favorite tonight").

  Desire is developed when the connection is made between a product and its guest benefit. Using visual appeal, speed appeal, or enticing, descriptive words increases a guest's desire for a product.

  Calling for *action* in a positive way and making the assumption that guests are interested in a product ("Can I take your dessert order now?" rather than "Are you going to have dessert?") moves the guest by asking for the order.

Point-of-Purchase (POP) Materials

Point-of-purchase materials are used to call guest attention to specific products. These often include: blackboards, posters, lifesize die cuts, table tents, and interesting containers filled with appropriate products, such as bottles of wine.

One industry expert offers the following pointers for using point-of-purchase materials (*2*):

- *Highlight fewer items more often.* Promotion experts agree that it is better to highlight the same products or services throughout the restaurant in various ways rather than offer too many different products or services, which might be confusing to guests.

- *Avoid clutter.* When point-of-purchase materials are overused, their messages get lost.

- *Use simple designs and easy-to-read lettering.* Guests appreciate attractive designs and print that is large and clear enough to read easily.

- *Create effective headlines.* Since four out of five guests never read beyond the headlines, they should contain the most important information.

- *Have a consistent format.* Guests should be able to get the message quickly.

- *Comply with legal requirements.* When brand names or trademarks appear in print, they require certain designations, such as © for copyright and ™ for trademark.

- *Illustrate the objective.* Liberal use of drawings, graphics, or photographs is suggested.

- *Don't cut corners on paper grade and print quality.* Guests connect these to the quality of the product offered.

- *Use artistic devices.* Contrasts such as black backgrounds, colored paper, and reversals draw guest attention.

- *Remove point-of-purchase materials as needed.* Out-of-date materials or those used too long detract from a facility's appearance and quality image.

Packaging

Packaging contributes to a product's appeal. It may consist of unusual presentation of a product through innovative size, shape, or color containers, unique serviceware, creative garnishes, special attractions, such as flambés in the dining room, or the use of the product as a room decoration. When well executed, packaging can make ordinary food look special, thus influencing the guest to purchase the item as well as enhancing the dining experience.

Restaurants also use packaging to differentiate their products from their competitors' products. Guests learn to associate types of packaging with specific facilities.

Restaurateurs carefully select which items to package based on their appeal and profitability. They also limit the number of items receiving special packaging, to avoid overwhelming guests and to control costs. Extra labor is frequently required to prepare packaging that is elaborate.

Sampling

Restaurants offer guests a sample of a new or highly profitable menu item as a promotional technique. Few people can resist a sample, especially if it is presented attractively by a friendly server. Samples influence guests to try new menu offerings, stimulate their appetites, and promote general goodwill. Samples are offered when guests are waiting for a table or after they are seated. Samples provided as appetizers encourage guests to purchase additional beverages. Perhaps, the greatest benefit of samples is that they make guests feel special, thus enhancing guest service.

Better-value Alternatives

Better-value alternatives or added-value alternatives refer to the practice of offering guests an alternative to a restaurant product that provides a better value. For instance, if an 8-ounce soft drink is available at 59 cents, a jumbo 16-ounce soft drink might be offered at 99 cents. Industry figures show that when this technique is used, an estimated 40 percent of guests will opt for the better value, thus leading to impressive sales increases.

Restaurants effectively use this technique when they offer several different sizes of popular items or combine menu items into a package that costs less than each of the items purchased separately. Guests perceive that the better-value alternatives are true bargains.

Strategies that Work

The strategies to attract guests discussed in this chapter are merely the basics. They must be applied imaginatively according to the needs of a particular facility. The industry has many examples of restaurateurs who have used their ingenuity to successfully attract a loyal clientele to their establishments. Here are just a few:

- One operator offers two types of restaurants in one facility to appeal to different market segments. There is a casual restaurant offering "Everything from escargot, tacos al carbon, and Chinese chicken salad to hamburgers, soups, and salads" (*11*). The second restaurant is more elaborate and serves gourmet entrées, such as stuffed chicken breast, rack of lamb, and unique pasta creations (*11*).

- An institutional foodservice company changed its image on several college campuses. In addition to offering traditional cafeteria service, the contract company installed "Pizza delivery outlets, Mexican and Chinese take-out operations, and vendor carts [selling] everything from bagels to hot dogs" (*8*). The contract company attracts new guests with these new services, including faculty and students who are living off-campus.

- A Hawaiian resort has an "Unusual ordering system that management says has become a point of notoriety" (*19*). There is no printed menu, instead, guests are escorted to a butchering area where they choose from a variety of meats and seafood. "The selections include local fishes, such as mahi mahi and opaka opaka; New York steak and prime rib, ordered by the ounce; and shellfish, such as tiger prawns. Each is cut and prepared to the customers' specifications" (*19*).

- Since many guests seem to enjoy a light meal and beverage in the late afternoon, some hotels have begun offering afternoon tea. Guests at one hotel relax in the lobby lounge and are served tea, small sandwiches, and assorted pastries on fine china. Entertainment is provided by a pianist or other musician. (*17*).

- A restaurant in New York purchased a 1978 Daimler limousine and offers it free-of-charge to guests on a first-come, first-served basis. The limousine is chauffeur-driven and is used to take guests anywhere they want within Manhattan. According to the owner, the strategy is highly successful. "The limousine is our way of making our guests' experience . . . a bit more enjoyable" (*22*).

- A casual theme restaurant in Pompano Beach, Florida has changed its strategy to attract an aging generation. According to the director of operations, "We're dealing with an older baby-boom generation. They want more comfort. So we've spaced the tables out a little more, the chairs are more comfortable, and the noise level has been controlled" (*14*).

- A celebrated New York restaurant is a mix of sophistication, elegance, and innovation. This luxury restaurant entices guests with five different menus daily, which change completely every three months. This, along with impeccable, personalized service has helped make the restaurant a favorite of the rich, the famous, and the powerful (*5*).

- Guests at one California restaurant enjoy meals prepared from recipes in detective Nero Wolfe's cookbook, while watching a play which ends with a murdered restaurant critic and "A plea from the police for help in solving the case" (*18*). Other restaurants give guests a more active role in murder mystery evenings—guests are asked to come dressed as their favorite detective story character and are given the chance to dramatize and solve a murder mystery.

- One restaurateur offers guests "networking" meals at various city restaurants. Guests pay a yearly fee which entitles them to discounted meals or complimentary products at participating restaurants, while they meet and dine with other members of the network. "Members are matched according to their professional responsibilities, cuisine and ambiance preferences, and lunch budgets" (*16*).

- Beautiful scenery enhances any dining experience. One Iowa restaurant offers fine dining with a luxurious, scenic train ride. The trip lasts several hours during which time, guests enjoy a beautiful view along with an elegant four-course, fixed-price dinner (*15*).

- A restaurant in Kansas City, Missouri attracts guests interested in wines by providing an enormous wine selection. According to the owner, "We take great pride in our extensive wine list. Not only are we interested in wine ourselves, but we get our guests involved in the selection of wines from our cellar" (*13*). Periodically, the restaurant invites regular guests to a wine tasting to help evaluate new wines. The serving staff is an essential part of the strategy. The owner states, "We hold monthly staff meetings, where they get a chance to taste and compare our new wines against some of the standards. They become quite knowledgeable. There's a big difference between someone who asks, 'Would you like wine with your meal?' and someone who can suggest the right wine for the occasion and the type of food" (*13*). While the restaurant does not offer special incentives to the staff for promoting wines, the staff realizes that wine sales increase check and tip size. In addition, promoting wines makes them feel professional.

- One California establishment significantly increased its sales by installing a "chocoholic bar" that offers a variety of unique desserts which change daily. The charge for the chocolate bar entitles guests to one visit to the buffet, where they may choose as many desserts as desired (*6*).

- A Detroit restaurant has also found that offering a variety of chocolate desserts can be lucrative. The restaurateur discovered that many guests do not order dessert "if there is no chocolate on the menu." The facility offers such delicacies as "Chocolate meringue tortes layered with fresh berries, nuts, and coconut sealed with a whipped cream-and-butter mixture and finally covered with a chocolate ganache [icing]" (*6*). Despite the fact that this type of dessert costs much more than usual dessert offerings, due to the expensive ingredients used and the excessive preparation time, guests demand it (*6*).

- Owners of a successful Illinois truck-stop have changed the fare they offer to keep pace with the "Increased numbers and diversification" of their clientele which includes tourists and local residents. Overhauling their menu from the usual "stick-to-your-ribs" variety, they added many new items including light finger foods and salads. In addition to highlighting specials, the new menu features historical information about the restaurant and the Indians who settled in central Illinois (*23*).

3

Providing Quality Service: The Human Connection

Where Does It Begin?

Caring, hospitable service has its roots in a company's corporate culture. It begins with the president or other head of an organization who is committed to people as well as to profit—leaders who recognize that an organization's purpose is to satisfy people on both sides of the counter. This concept has its origins in management's values and beliefs. It is manifested by low employee turnover rates and permeates and influences the daily actions of the entire staff in large and small ways. It underlies the selection and development of all personnel—from corporate staff to front-line employees.

The commitment to quality service is usually found in a business' mission statement, operational philosophy, or restaurant policy. *It's up front,* as in the sample restaurant mission statement in Chart 3.1. Companies include various service principles in their

45

mission statements. Some of these are:

- Make the organization a challenging and rewarding place for people to grow and work.

- "Impress guests" by exceeding their expectations of quality, cleanliness, value, and caring service.

- Provide employees and guests with personal attention "In a way that lends dignity to guests and bespeaks pride on the part of the establishment" (*32*).

Chart 3.1. Sample Mission Statement

We will be a viable, moderately priced, full service, family dining restaurant chain with two primary focuses: financial success and the welfare of those who contribute to that success, specifically:

To provide guests with unique value through quality food and beverage, service, friendliness, and care within a clean and pleasant atmosphere.

> Given the choice of product and service at an identical price, the guest would prefer that of our restaurant.

To provide a high quality of work life, pride and the opportunity for personal development for all its employees regardless of position.

> Given the choice of identical financial compensation with another organization, employees would choose to remain at our restaurant.

To be recognized by suppliers as a company that appreciates their products and services and one that learns from them.

> Given a supplier cannot, at some point, satisfy the demands of all its customers, it would give preference to our restaurant.

To be considered an outstanding business citizen in every community in which we operate.

> We would carry out our normal business activities in such a way as to make contributions to the quality of life in these communities.

- "Make pleasurable dining affordable"(*30*).

- Offer "Thoughtful, complete, attentive service with relaxed efficiency" (*31*).

- Abide by the "Golden Rule"—treat guests as you would like to be treated.

- Provide "Complete responsiveness to the desires of our customers" (*11*).

- Optimize the quality of hospitality that each guest receives from employees (*33*).

The mission or philosophy must manifest itself in job designs, budgets, position descriptions, personnel selection, bonuses, incentives, reviews, and most of all, in day-by-day feedback that acknowledges people for providing quality service. A written service philosophy arising from the company's mission, policies, and rules is a vital tool to provide employees on all levels of the organization a single purpose— *guest satisfaction.*

There are only two levels of employees. First, those who serve the guest; and second, those who serve those who serve the guest. All personnel must be aware of guest needs, wants, and priorities and that their primary function is to satisfy these through the dining experience. It is a must for any establishment and is the basis for all restaurant strategies, policies, and procedures. A sample restaurant service policy appears in Chart 3.2.

Chart 3.2. Sample Restaurant Service Philosophy

To provide each guest a quality dining experience by providing quality food and quality service in a clean, well maintained, and pleasant surrounding.

Source: The Ground Round, Inc., (*34*).

Service Relates to All Levels of the Organizational Structure

Today's restaurant companies have complex organizational structures with a myriad of job titles and functions. All employees, no matter what their positions may be, have roles that pertain to guest service.

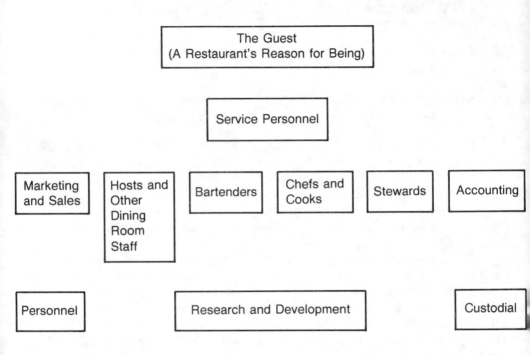

Decisions concerning the three aspects of service (delivery systems, standardized experience procedures, and interpersonal relationships) are made at the top level of the restaurant hierarchy. Executives must make policy decisions based on guests' needs, wants, and expectations. As restaurants grow and evolve into multi-unit companies, executives typically have little contact with guests. They must depend on marketing research and front-line personnel (employees in the facility who interact with guests) to provide information on guest satisfaction and dissatisfaction. If communication between policy makers and front-line employees is ineffective, there will be a gap between the development and delivery of vital service policies and procedures.

To avoid such gaps, companies formalize the feedback process between executives and front-line personnel. Organizations use both guest and employee audits on monthly and quarterly bases to monitor the attitudes and opinions about service, as well as about food, beverages, cleanliness, price/value benefit, and other factors. Those employees who have no direct contact with guests are assigned a role which is supportive to those who do. Based upon survey outcomes, they are involved in the strategies, policies, and procedures that facilitate guest service. These are the guidelines that specify how an operation will achieve its service philosophy. They are needed to ensure that a restaurant provides a consistently high level of service, and they facilitate communication between management and front-line service personnel. Ideally, a system is designed so that, "The organization exists to serve the needs of the people who are serving the customer" (7).

Employees need to be aware of company strategies, policies, and procedures to maintain the company's standard of guest service. Strategies, policies, and procedures should always be in writing and appear in a company's operations and training manuals.

Personnel: Their Service Role

Since all personnel, not only front-line employees, carry out the strategies, policies, and procedures that result in exceptional guest service, it's critical to understand their service roles.

Policy Makers

Policy makers are frequently called the organization's executives, whether at company headquarters or on-site. They depend on feedback from guests and employees to develop the facility's service philosophy, strategy, and standard policies and procedures. They ensure that these are carried out to meet company goals. Through these activities, they are responsible, although indirectly, for providing guest service. As organizations have grown, "Too many firms have lost sight of the fact that their success hinges on the guest being placed at the summit of the pyramid and being carefully heeded in menu selections, pricing, merchandising, and every other aspect of the business" (24). They all too often become driven by quantitative results, rather than by guests' needs. Many executives fall into the trap of spending too much of their time with financial reports.

In addition to policy makers, other personnel at the corporate level have critical service-related responsibilities. Food and beverage directors are responsible for creating a menu with guest appeal; purchasing personnel are responsible for procuring the highest quality products at the lowest price and in the correct amounts, so that facilities do not run out of food and supplies; marketing personnel are responsible for determining who the guests are and what services they want or expect, and for planning advertising and promotional campaigns that will create a greater perceived benefit and bring consumers into the establishment; and personnel managers establish programs to identify friendly, effective people, teach them how to provide caring guest service, and provide motivational programs that will reward them for hospitable guest service.

These executives' support of front-line personnel ultimately effects quality service in the restaurant. "You can train all you like at the lower levels of an organization, but if top and middle management do not [financially support or] encourage people [through incentives based upon] newly learned skills and give them feedback (positive and negative) those new skills will soon disappear" (*13*). A training fundamental is that people tend to do that for which they are rewarded and to avoid that which carries the risk of punishment.

Division Staff

In larger organizations, there are middle-management employees at corporate headquarters who work in various divisions such as purchasing, advertising, or menu development, or who are responsible for regional operations. Division employees are a communications link between higher-level executives and facility staff, and thus, are the key link in the service chain. They usually have been developed from within and have first-hand experience in guest service.

A number of successful operations require all executives and middle-level managers to work at least one week each year in a restaurant.

Restaurant Managers

Restaurant managers are the key to quality service. Managers have more influence on the quality of the staff's service attitude and behavior than all others. Service relates to all of a manager's responsibilities. Thus, service-conscious managers are the key to having service-minded employees. To foster hospitable service, managers (*32*):

- *Act as role models.* This is perhaps the single most important function of a manager. What managers do speaks louder than what they say. They value their employees and guests. It is through this modeling that they demonstrate every second they are on the job how they foster crew cooperation to provide outstanding service. They demonstrate directly and indirectly the components of excellent service.

- *Hire competent staff.* They have "people sense" and make the right hiring decisions. According to Elton Statler, the three most important factors to a successful hotel are "location, location, location." Using this approach, the three most important factors in successful service are "Selection, selection, selection." In addition to role modeling, managers must identify individuals with "People skills" and hire them. No matter how much modeling or training is provided, a service person who does not enjoy people and cannot demonstrate enthusiasm for them will be unable to give hospitable service.

- *Respect employees.* They are fair in all their actions and, most of all, demonstrate a deep-seated respect for their team. It has been said, "All employees come with a brain at no extra charge, so why not use it."

- *Communicate with staff.* They know that employees must understand exactly what is expected of them and have the linguistic ability to affect the right behaviors.

- *Train employees.* Managers must know how to train employees so that they are unconsciously efficient in the necessary functional tasks. Outstanding service personnel have their tasks so "habitized" that they can focus more on the individual needs of their guests. Managers explain, demonstrate, let employees try (and make their mistakes), redirect their behavior, and "habitize" employees' skills so that they may perform their duties in such a way as to exceed guests' expectations.

- *Coach from the dining room floor.* Successful managers spend time in the dining area where they can provide moment-to-moment feedback on employee service. They set a standard of decorum for the rest of the staff, greet guests, and remember and use their names when they enter the establishment. They thank guests for their patronage and invite them to return. When managers are in the dining area, they can spot and correct potential problems before they become major. The manager's job is to assist the service crews in creating a bond of loyalty with the guests. They show the crew what good service looks like.

Coaching also means that managers provide positive reinforcement. They tell people when they have done "it" (good service) right. They recognize good performance and praise excellence. They acknowledge employees who do their jobs well. This makes staff feel that they are an integral part of the success of the operation, increases staff loyalty, and ultimately leads to greater guest satisfaction.

- *Give constructive criticism.* Managers know that employees cannot remain enthusiastic about a task unless they are challenged by it. In order to assist their crew in becoming better workers, managers must make staff aware of their mistakes and help them change improper behavior. No matter how much managers care for their crew, the adage applies—"Love without discipline isn't."

- *Get the most out of service staff.* They recognize employees as individuals and credit those who provide hospitable service. This results in better guest service. At one successful operation, the manager sends cards to employees on their birthdays and on their yearly anniversaries with the company. This manager states, "I believe that the first and last measure in maintaining a loyal staff (and clientele) is personal, concerned attention to the individual" (20).

- *Facilitate service by supervising and adapting systems and procedures so the crew has no obstacles to providing good service.* Competent managers are aware that well-designed systems are vital to achieve the company's service philosophy. However, no system is perfect and even the best of systems must adapt with change. They recognize that their systems should be, "Designed for the convenience of the guest rather than the convenience of the organization. The physical facilities, policies, procedures, methods, and communications processes all say to the guest, 'This apparatus is here to meet your needs'" (7). Successful managers ensure that a facility meets established standards at all times and that all necessary resources are available when needed.

- *Maintain clarity of purpose and priorities and convey these to the crew.* They remind all employees in words and in actions that guests are the operation's first concern and that systems and procedures are not the end-all; they are the methods used to achieve guest satisfaction.

- *Schedule for sufficient coverage.* Competent managers identify minimum staffing standards. They recognize that understaffed restaurants may provide the short-term reward of a low labor cost percentage, but they cannot provide long-term quality service. Able managers establish standard ratios of employee hours to guest transactions and stick to them. To support their managers, service organizations need to avoid rewarding managers who show higher profits because they operate at below-standard service expense. When they do so over time, the quality of service declines.

- *Attend to details.* They know that it is the smallest details that make a great restaurant stand apart from its competition.

- *Recognize regular guests.* Patrons frequent an establishment because they know and trust its manager and crew. They believe they have a bond that will ensure a satisfactory dining experience. When the manager (or other assigned person) recognizes and welcomes these guests, the guests know their loyalty is appreciated and they will be given personalized service.

- *Have complaint procedures.* Restaurant production and service require much human judgement. Since humans err, problems do occur. Unfortunately, guests do not always verbalize their complaints. Managers must be skilled at reading facial expressions, interpreting body language, and noticing when guests do not finish their meals. They must identify problems before the guests leave the facility. Having standard procedures to handle complaints enables managers to deal expediently with recognized problems and to satisfy their guests.

- *Evaluate the operation.* They must monitor operating results, particularly guest counts, average checks, food to beverage ratios, and costs. Good managers remain flexible, and make changes in accordance with company policies and procedures.

Staff Employees

There are two categories of staff positions: 1) contact employees (such as hosts/hostesses, bartenders, captains, servers, and bus personnel) who serve the guests' needs directly; and 2) staff who support the contact employees (such as kitchen, accounting, and engineering personnel). Although, in most cases, support staff do not come in contact with guests, they do provide a vital service function. They perform the tasks necessary for the smooth operation of the facility. Unfortunately, some establishments concentrate on the performance of these tasks rather than on guest satisfaction that results when these tasks are performed effectively. Since facility success depends on the guest's experience, *every job duty must be performed to ensure guest satisfaction.*

Staff are responsible for providing quality, professional service based on performance standards which are designed to satisfy the guests' needs. There's more to professional service than simply being polite. It entails procedures with measurable performance standards. Poor service detracts from the highest quality food. Even when it is "... an ordinary meal, presented in an undistinguished setting, it can be transformed [by good service] into a special pleasure"(22). Personalized attention and caring service mean that employees are hospitable and manage the guest's experience. They:

- *Acknowledge guests on arrival with a hospitable greeting.* The "eye," the "smile," and the "word," are the three keys to a warm and genuine welcome. All three behaviors should occur before the guest is forced to become the initiator of hospitality. The antithesis of a hospitable greeting is to ignore guests at any point during their dining experience, whether it is when they enter the facility, when they are seated, or when they require assistance.

- *Anticipate and attend to guests' needs.* Guests should not have to search for an employee when they want service. Some facilities use an "expediter system" which allows service personnel to remain on the dining room floor while special delivery "runners" bring prepared orders to tables.

- *Provide knowledgeable information.* Guests may be dining at a restaurant because they want to try new types of foods or beverages. Employees should be able to provide customers with requested information about food preparation or ingredients used, they should be able to give food selection recommendations.

Employees are also responsible for making and keeping loyal guests—an important revenue source for any operation. In addition to the capital generated by their patronage, the word-of-mouth promotion satisfied guests provide is invaluable. Personalized service is a key component for ensuring guest loyalty and must be apparent at critical moments, or "HOT (Hospitality Opportunity Times) spots" during the dining experience. These critical moments vary for different types of service styles but typically include when guests (32):

- *Make a reservation.* Whether reservations are taken by telephone, handled by mail, or made by guests at the facility, how they are handled sets the tone for an entire facility. Employees should attend to what the reserver wants and respond in an appropriate, courteous, and helpful manner. Even if the restaurant is booked at the requested day or time, the employee should be apologetic and encourage the guest to "try us again." Turning down a reservation request in an abrupt or otherwise discourteous manner is a sure way to lose future business.

- *Enter the property.* There is only one time to make a first impression, and it does count. A facility must be in "hospitable order." The outside and entry of the establishment should be attractive, well-maintained, and spotless for both aesthetic and security reasons. Parking areas should be clearly marked and have proper lighting. Menus should be available for guests to read. A comfortable guest waiting area is important.

- *Have their first contact with an employee.* Guests should be greeted immediately. The greeting is an indication of all the good things that are going to happen to them during their meal period. The person at the front of the establishment should be a trained, enthusiastic greeter. Whether this employee is a parking valet, host or hostess, manager, order taker, or other staff member, attentive and pleasant greetings are a must.

- *Are seated.* Guests should be seated immediately if seats are available. If guests are to seat themselves, there should be signs telling them to do so. When guests are ignored, management has "Lost control of their dining experience"(*14*).

- *Have special requests.* Managers should always be listening for opportunities to provide guests with special assistance. Whether guests need help in being seated in some particular area (e.g., a quiet corner, a non-smoking area, etc.) or want a menu item specially prepared, hospitality-conscious establishments accommodate them. These are the HOT spots. Occasionally, when special requests cannot be handled, guests should be promptly and courteously informed and some form of compensation provided. It is a nice added touch when employees offer alternative solutions to the problem.

- *Await service recognition.* Guests should be greeted by a service person within a specified period (one to two minutes). When this is not possible at peak periods, guests should be informed that the service person is aware of their presence and will be with them shortly. If facilities keep guests waiting more than five minutes, they should reexamine their scheduling policies.

- *Order their food.* Taking guest orders is a skill. Servers must know all the products offered so they can answer guests' questions and make suggestions. Usually orders are taken from children and women in the party first. When taking orders, all special requests or instructions must be noted.

- *Are served food.* Guests appreciate when servers remember what has been ordered by whom and place the food before the right guest. Many restaurants have an order policy which begins at a certain point no matter what table is served. Shortly after guests have tasted their food, it is advisable for servers to ensure that the quality is satisfactory.

- *Use restrooms.* Restrooms in poor condition reflect on the restaurant's attention to detail in all private places in the facility. Restrooms should be spotless and equipped with necessary supplies. Properly maintained restrooms show guests that the restaurant cares about their comfort. An inspection chart specifying time of inspection and the supervisor's initials are frequently used as a means to audit this attention.

- *Have complaints.* Complaints need to be handled immediately, politely, and to the guests' satisfaction.

- *Pay their bills and leave the restaurant.* The last impression a guest receives is almost as important as the first impression. Appropriately handling payment and thanking all guests for their business is a must.

Profile of Guest-oriented Service Personnel

In addition to being able to form a bond with others based on friendliness, those who serve guests directly require characteristics necessary to accomplish the service task. These qualities include:

- *Empathy.* The ability to feel and reflect the mood of others.

- *A desire for the acceptance of others.* The willingness to go out of the way for others to gain their approval.

- *An effective communication style.* The ability to think clearly and respond to others with the right words, facial expressions, and body language.

- *High energy level.* The ability to sustain physical and mental performance for long periods.

- *Tolerance.* The maturity to sustain emotional control during stressful periods.

- *Enjoyment of the unknown.* The appreciation and enjoyment of managing unforeseen situations.

- *Cooperative personality.* The talent of working with others and being able to sacrifice personal desires for team goals.

- *Sense of humor.* The ability to laugh and see humor in one's own mistakes.

- *Courtesy and tact.* Responding with the right words in the right way at the right time.

- *Pleasing appearance.* Possession of the attributes that enhance the dining experience for guests.

People with these qualities are "conscious competents" because they make a conscious effort to perform their duties with a positive attitude. There are four classifications of worker competency:

- *Unconscious Incompetents.* Employees who lack the basic qualities and skill competencies to accomplish the necessary position tasks. For example, these would include people who are required to perform certain bookkeeping functions but have poor quantitative aptitude, or those who must meet and persuade the public but lack empathy and language skills.

- *Conscious Incompetents.* Employees who have all the necessary competencies except for the desire to accomplish their tasks. They can perform, but they will not.

- *Unconscious Competents.* Employees with all the necessary competencies, including skills, knowledge, and confidence. They are winners and need little if any training, instruction, or coaching.

- *Conscious Competents.* Employees who have all the necessary job qualifications and competencies except for specific skill, knowledge, and confidence. They can be trained for skills, taught for knowledge, and coached for confidence. Most people fall into this classification.

Recruiting Competent Personnel

Restaurant operators often have difficulty recruiting service-oriented people. A 1986 *Restaurants & Institutions* survey of fast-service, and institutional operators found that almost three-quarters of operators considered it difficult to find quality hourly and managerial workers (*29*). Popular recruiting sources include:

- *Present employees.* The best way to find high quality personnel is through current quality service employees who may have friends or relatives who are looking for employment (*21*).

- *Schools.* In addition to general foodservice programs in training centers, high schools, and vocational schools, there are now 571 college-level programs in hotel, restaurant, and institutional management (*28*). Career days or interviews scheduled through school placement offices provide the opportunity to reach students interested in foodservice careers. In addition, some operators place advertisements in school newspapers.

- *Reward systems.* Some facilities offer rewards to employees or guests whose recommendations result in hiring a new employee. Sometimes, these rewards are two-stage: 1) when the employee is hired; and 2) when the employee remains on the job for a specified period (usually 3 to 6 months).

- *Newspapers and industry publications.* Newspapers and industry publications are among the most traditional means of recruiting both entry-level and experienced workers. "Thirty-three percent of employees seriously committed to the foodservice industry initiate their job searches by reading recruitment ads in trade publications" (*19*).

- *Employment agencies.* Some agencies specialize in placement of hospitality industry personnel (*5*).

- *Guests.* Many companies use signs and posters inside the restaurant to recruit crew members. Some operations are using bag stuffers, table tents, and placemats to inform guests about job opportunities. During a recent labor shortage, order takers at one fast-service chain asked guests if they were looking for a job (*12, 18, 21*).

- *Bulletin boards.* Bulletin boards in local supermarkets and community centers are especially useful for attracting teens, mothers, and older people who are interested in part-time employment (*18*).

- *Radio and television.* Electronic media are being used to reach large audiences. Recently, one restaurant chain company "Produced the first full-length television commercial specifically geared to recruitment" of senior citizens (*25*).

The Coaching of Conscious Competents

Although service personnel have been selected because they are conscious competents, they require training, education, and confidence to become professionals. They need to acquire the knowledge and skills and have the reassurance of knowing when they provide guests with pleasurable dining experiences. It is best when they view themselves as more than the sum of their job descriptions. They need to understand that they are customer-makers—marketing or sales representatives responsible for exceeding guests' expectations.

All conscious competents, even those who already possess skills, can be further developed professionally. They must know the guests' desires, the restaurant's service policies and procedures, and the benefits of available products. Managers can rely on ten rules for educating, training, coaching, and evaluating employees to develop their professionalism.

A Ten-step Coaching Procedure for Developing Conscious Competents

STEP 1: All personnel must become members of a team with the common purpose of guest satisfaction. Employees need to be assured that they are joining a winning organization. They should be led to understand that no individual can accomplish the goal alone—the whole team is necessary.

Building on the restaurant's mission statement, dedication to high standards, and traditions of quality guest service is the first step toward achieving the goal.

STEP 2: Ensure that employees know their job functions and understand why their jobs are important to the team objective. Team members should be aware that the team is not for everyone (i.e. cuts are made, and they are made early in the game). They must distinguish between the two critical player lineups: 1) the contact personnel who are the front line of guest service; and 2) the support staff who exist to support contact personnel; but they should recognize that everyone in the facility has a key role in providing satisfaction by cooperating to build team spirit.

STEP 3: Provide employees with challenging, defined, and measurable performance standards. First, they must know what a "good job" looks like and the professional standards it entails. Their actions should be based on performance measures. For example, the standard for a professional team in a fast-service restaurant might be to expedite a guest order in less than 60 seconds at the counter or in less that 45 seconds at the drive-through. There might be individual performance standards as well, perhaps based on time or quality of individual performance. Each task should be assigned a series of challenges for which performance standards are stepped up. As employees achieve various levels, they should be publicly recognized in some way.

STEP 4: Educate and train employees. Product knowledge is critical to maximize guest satisfaction. When servers know the items on the menu, they are able to help guests more fully enjoy their experience. The information necessary includes: recipe knowledge (how items are prepared); service times; nutritional information; and complementary foods and beverages. The key is less the information than the guest benefit associated with the knowledge (i.e., the recipe is important to help describe the taste treat experience). Professional service personnel are not just order takers, they must answer guests' questions, solve guest problems, and apply suggestive-selling principles.

Employees should be able to state product benefits. "It may be nice for an employee to know that Alsace is a small wine-producing region on the border of France, but the restaurant operator should be concerned that employees can use that information in [explaining why the wine has a specific and unique taste] . . . The principle is simple: knowledge for knowledge sake is not an efficient goal of training" (*33*).

Also, employees must be able to provide new information to the guest. New knowledge is the foundation for employee enthusiasm, which is contagious and is passed on to the guest. New knowledge enthusiastically passed on is the basis for word-of-mouth promotion.

Successful operators make new knowledge an integral part of their personnel development programs. For example, at one fine restaurant offering unconventional foods, servers meet individually with the manager and spend several days working in the kitchen before they are assigned a station (26).

Conducting wine- or food-tasting sessions are also popular means of educating employees. Such instruction should be accompanied by suggestive selling and other merchandising strategies. One industry executive who conducts wine-tasting seminars for service personnel includes information on proper glassware, serving sizes, complementary menu items, and possible ways to promote wine (10).

Eighty percent of restaurants use on-the-job training as the main method to train hourly employees. Others conduct training programs on-premises or at an outside location.

The service techniques and performance standards should become so "habitized" that they are delivered without thinking. The thinking should be focused on satisfying the guest's personal needs. A metaphor that best explains the objective is driving an automobile. The driver should not be concentrating on how to start, steer, and stop the car; rather, attention should be given to getting to the destination as efficiently and effectively as possible. The well-trained staff should be focusing on the destination, i.e., on guest satisfaction, rather than on the techniques for writing orders, carrying trays, placing food and drink on tables, or billing a guest. Hospitality is best delivered when service employees concentrate on the guests' needs rather than on the service process. The ultimate in "Customer satisfaction depends on each employee performing his or her job [so well as to exceed] the customer's expectations. Any employee who performs below standard becomes the weakest link in the 'service chain'" (3).

"The best way to insure that [a] restaurant is creating an environment of hospitality is to teach and train using a system that emphasizes" (33) individual need, identification, and recognition, i.e., remembering names. The training procedure is as follows: 1) orient; 2) describe; 3) demonstrate; 4) practice; 5) acknowledge good performance; and 6) correct and redirect improper performance. It is most effective when carried out under the guidance of training managers and other training personnel, since not all people are qualified trainers.

Chart 3.3 shows one approach to the training process); while Chart 3.4 shows one example of a job breakdown used in the process.

STEP 5: Provide players with successful experiences. Personnel should be rewarded early in the learning process. This reward may simply be recognition for doing the job partly right. All trainees need to be told when they have done tasks correctly to reinforce good performances and build confidence. This feedback is critical to good training. A distinction is made between feedback and praise. Feedback is recognizing good performance when a learner does a task or part of a task correctly. Praise is the enthusiastic and public response given for excellent performance.

STEP 6: Reinforce ("habitize") the basics. Employees strive to do their best when they know their work will be inspected. The basics of guest service should be reinforced daily. It is critical that restaurant managers be "on the floor" attending to guest satisfaction. They should reinforce individual and team performance as often as possible. A crew will respond to the behavior of the manager far more than to what the manager or policy manual says.

STEP 7: Give individual, formal appraisals. Let employees know how well they are performing on designated occasions. These performance evaluations should be designed for two-way communication. They are used to identify the strengths of personnel and help them develop professionally.

Performance evaluations should be productive, valuable experiences for both the company and the employee. In productive evaluations, evaluators (*1, 4, 8*):

- *Stick to the issues.* The purpose of an evaluation is to discuss present and future job performance. It is not the appropriate time for a discussion concerning salary, scheduling, or other work- or non-work-related topics.

- *Conduct evaluations in a comfortable atmosphere.* Evaluations are more effective when both the manager and the employee are as relaxed as possible. Since evaluations are personal, they should be conducted in private and not be interrupted. Employees should be discouraged from discussing their evaluations with other employees (except during team evaluations).

- *Discuss work behaviors that need improvement.* Sometimes evaluators are uncomfortable discussing substandard behaviors, so they use the "sandwich method" of evaluation (compliment, criticize,

---

Chart 3.3. One Training Approach

- *Determine the job duties employees are expected to perform.* Prepare a list of tasks for each job. Be sure to include input from the most professional service personnel on the team. Typical duties for service personnel might be listed as:

Approaching the guest.

Greeting the guest.

Saying the bonding remark.

Giving a friendly suggestion.

Taking the order.

Writing the order check.

Communicating the order to production.

Picking up the order.

Serving the order.

Ensuring quality satisfaction.

Providing the unexpected extra.

Taking the reorder or final order.

Preparing the bill.

Presenting the guest check.

Collecting payment.

Saying goodbye and thank you.

Managing the special guest.

Handling a complaint.

- *Break down each job duty into sequential steps.* Job breakdowns are detailed lists of all steps required to complete each task.

Chart 3.3. One Training Approach (continued)

- *Explain how hospitable behavior and product knowledge relate to task completion.* Then, use job breakdowns as lesson plans.

- *List all the new words, definitions, and pronunciations required to implement the task.*

- *Make certain everyone knows where all materials are located and how to use them.*

- *Conduct training sessions.* Training sessions require planning. One-to-one sessions conducted at the facility are preferred. Training sessions have several steps:

  Trainer selection. Most training programs require trainers skilled in the job duties they are teaching. As a rule, inexperienced persons cannot effectively train others and using them as trainers creates below standard performance.

  Scripting the training. All training steps should be written down in learning steps. Descriptive pictures should be used wherever possible.

  Determine where training will be conducted. When possible, conduct training at work stations where employees will be expected to carry out tasks after training is complete.

  Schedule the training period. Determine when and how long sessions will be. Sessions should be scheduled during slower periods and when trainers have sufficient time to prepare. Forty-five minute sessions are recommended.

  Assemble training materials. List the training materials needed for each session on job breakdown lists. Gather these materials before the session to save time.

  Incorporate the use of all senses in the teaching process. Learning tools are enhanced when trainees must use all their senses—seeing, hearing, smelling, tasting, and feeling (doing).

  Keep to the purpose of the session. Tell employees which tasks will be taught and why they are important. "Help trainees understand how the skill relates to their total responsibilities and how their work contributes to the overall goals of the restaurant. Emphasize

---

Chart 3.3. One Training Approach (continued)

[guest satisfaction] as a major goal and stress the fact that hospitality should influence how every skill is performed in a restaurant."

Demonstrate and explain. Have trainees read the job breakdown. Next, demonstrate how to complete the task step-by-step. Explain the importance of each step, and how to perform it correctly.

Give trainees an opportunity to complete the task. Have trainees demonstrate and explain each step of the task

Let trainees practice. Trainees become proficient when they are allowed to practice.

Begin training in a no-risk situation. Learning is less likely in stress situations. Permit learners to make mistakes when there is no risk of losing customers.

Evaluate performance. Feedback is important. Trainees need to be coached. Provide additional training if employees still have difficulty performing tasks after practicing and praise trainees when they are successful. "When a trainee strays from the prescribed procedures, compliment them on what they have learned to do that is meeting the standards, and then pleasantly review the procedures that have gone off-course. This procedure will result in overall improvement of the employee's performance and the development of a positive attitude toward training."

Teach a few job breakdowns in each training period. Don't attempt to teach employees all necessary tasks in one training session. Employees will retain more information if they are not overwhelmed by the amount of information presented.

Source: Training for Hospitality, (*33*).

Chart 3.4. Job Breakdown: Taking Guest Orders

Task: Taking guest food orders
Prerequisite: Seating guests / menu presentation
Equipment: Guest check, pen

What to Do and Standard	How to Do It	Additional Information
1. Approach the table (3 minutes after seating, maximum).	Stand erect. Look at the guests, smile, and greet them pleasantly. Introduce yourself. If you know the guests' last names, use them as you greet the guests. Be courteous.	You win the table by your first contact when you are pleasant and personable. Read the party motivation. You may have to wait for a break in the conversation. Do not interrupt guest conversations to tend to a guest's obvious needs.
2. Take the cocktail order.	Provide a "choice" question. "Are you ready to order your cocktail now (implied) or would you like a little more time?" Suggest the cocktail of the week. Be sure to get complete details of the order, such as on-the-rocks, straight-up, or extra olives. Remember who ordered what cocktail.	Do not ask a yes or no question. "Are you going to have cocktails tonight?" Most guests know which drinks they prefer. Be prepared to make suggestions if appropriate. Do not push your personal preferences. Listen for the "qualified yes," "absolute yes," "qualified no," or "absolute no." Do not react negatively when a guest has an unusual drink request.
3. Serve cocktails (within 5 minutes of order).	Place a cocktail napkin before each guest. Serve all beverages	Knowing who ordered what shows that you care about the or-

Chart 3.4. Job Breakdown: Taking Guest Orders (continued)

What to Do and Standard	How to Do It	Additional Information
	from the left when possible. Place cocktail glasses on napkins. Do not ask who ordered what drink. As each drink is served, call it by name, such as scotch and water, double martini, or kir on-the-rocks.	der. Guests feel the special treatment when you repeat their orders as you serve their drinks.
4. Deliver drink stimulator food to table (within 3 minutes).	Explain complimentary food. Ask about satisfaction.	Look for reorder possibility.
5. Check back for a second cocktail (5 to 8 minutes or when drinks are two-thirds consumed).	"Are you ready for another yet?" If "Yes," bring the second round following the same procedures as the first round. Remove all first-round empty glasses and napkins. Set new napkins and serve the drinks. If "No", then ask "Are you ready to order now?"	Replace ashtrays. The third round is not to be encouraged. The policy of the restaurant is to control beverage alcohol consumption so as not to create an abuse condition. A third round may be accepted, but move to take food orders as soon as possible. If any risk of intoxication exists, notify the manager.
6. Take the food order.	Explain the chef's specialties of the day. Ask if there are any questions. Answer any questions. Take orders beginning with children and women when possible. Then proceed to male guests. Suggest appropriate appetizers, soups, or salads to help guests	Guests expect you to know about the food. When you are asked a question and do not know the answer, do not bluff. Explain that you will find out immediately. Inquire, then go back and tell the guest. Suggesting menu items helps a hesitant guest make a sat-

Chart 3.4. Job Breakdown: Taking Guest Orders (continued)

What to Do and Standard	How to Do It	Additional Information
	plan a complete meal. Be sure to inform guests of the approximate cooking times for selections requiring an extra wait.	isfactory decision. It also creates sales. Communication during this very important step is as critical as order taking. It should be "experience planning." Reinforce the suitability of the guest's order.
7. Take the wine order.	Ask: "Have you chosen a wine?" or, "May I help you select a wine?" When you are asked to help, ask whether guests prefer red or white, dry or semi-sweet, to get some idea of their preferences. Then, point out two or three choices that have the desired characteristics. Excuse yourself from the table and state that you will be right back with the first course.	Know the wine list. Always be careful to recognize those guests who are unused to selecting wines. Be prepared to coach them through a selection process that will meet their needs. Experienced wine drinkers usually know what they want to order and will not expect much assistance. This is not the time to feed your ego by demonstrating your technical wine knowledge. This might intimidate the guest. Be confident, but at the same time, be courteous. Encourage guests to use bin numbers rather than risk mispronunciation. Know your pronunciation.

Source: *Training for Hospitality*, (*33*).

compliment) or they downplay problems. "It is unlikely that any improvement will be made when the manager is unable to confront an employee's shortcoming for fear of making the employee 'feel bad' " (8).

- *Listen to the employee.* Part of an effective evaluation is the employee's self-evaluation. Self-evaluations encourage two-way communication and provide employees with an opportunity to tell management about their strengths and areas that need developing.

- *Set goals for future performance.* This is the primary objective of performance evaluations. The evaluator and the employee should determine how the employee's performance can be improved, and then set performance goals.

- *Continue to coach.* Employees should understand that the goals defined during the evaluation are challenges, and that the manager is confident that the employee's performance will improve.

STEP 8: Encourage employee teams to help solve problems through team self-evaluation. One of the keys to team building is displaying trust and respect in the players as a team. The people closest to the problem opportunity often have the best solutions. The terminology for this problem opportunity-solving technique is "quality circles." The more input employees have concerning their job duties, the greater their commitment to decisions that are made. The principle behind this concept is that no one works as hard as the *owner* (including the owner of an idea).

STEP 9: Let the team see the scoreboard. Measurement is a key to motivating. Two of the most important results to be measured are 1) the guest counts; and 2) the average check. The most effective period is seven days.

STEP 10: Do not overcoach. Conscious competents are "naturals." They are usually gifted at service, and often break with convention to achieve guest satisfaction.

Rewarding Employee Service Performance

How employees are rewarded for their work affects not only productivity, but the quality of service as well. Of course, tangible rewards, including wages, tips, and benefits, are important. But, intangible rewards, such as praise and job satisfaction, do count.

Wages

Traditionally, employee wages in the foodservice industry have been low in comparison to manufacturing and professional positions. But, the picture in changing. The industry has had to deal with the following factors:

- The diminishing labor supply (teens, immigrants).

- High employee turnover.

- The public view that restaurant pay is low, the hours long and undesirable, the stress level is high, and the work is not challenging.

- The low status of service positions.

Today, many operators are offering more competitive wages in order to attract skilled labor and decrease turnover. Salaries and benefits for employees vary throughout the industry depending on the location and type of facility. According to one study, 65.5 percent of fast-service operators, 71.4 percent of full-service operators, and 91.7 percent of institutional operators pay hourly workers more than the minimum wage (29). Front-line personnel in dining room facilities in this country receive additional compensation in the form of tips. Incorporating a service charge on the guest's bill, a European practice, is also done, but on a limited basis.

Benefits

When it comes to frequently offered benefits, a recent survey in *Restaurants & Institutions* found that (27):

- Slightly more than 84 percent of companies offer unit managers medical insurance.

- The percentages for assistant managers, chefs, and cooks are 83.6, 78.1, and 47.1 percent respectively.

- Approximately three-quarters of operators offer unit managers, assistant managers, and chefs free or discounted meals or lodgings. Slightly more than one-half of operators offer these benefits to cooks.

- More than one-half of operators provide unit managers and assistant managers with disability or dental insurance.

Another survey found that the types of added benefits hourly workers receive vary with the type of establishment and whether they are full-time or part-time workers (29):

- Fast-service operators give employees who work on high volume days additional time off and give competent employees more hours and responsibilities.

- Full-service operators offer chefs certification training and offer attendance incentives.

- Institutional operators offer scholarships for younger employees. Older employees typically receive some type of benefits package.

Intangible Benefits

Adequate compensation alone is not enough to motivate employees to provide quality service. The quality of life on the job is extremely important. The Labor Relations Institute of New York surveyed employees to determine what they wanted from their work. The employees responded with the following (1):

- Interesting work.

- Full appreciation of work done.

- Feeling of being in on things.

- Job security.

- Promotion and growth in the organization.

- Good working conditions.

- Personal loyalty to employees.

- Sympathetic help with personal problems.

- Tactful discipline.

A second study found that, "People who are challenged by their jobs, who are able to communicate about them, and who have a sense of accomplishment have a higher level of job satisfaction" (1).

Incentives

Meeting both monetary and emotional employee needs is necessary to maximize job satisfaction. Satisfied employees are motivated, have a personal interest in the success of the operation, and receive job satisfaction by working with operators who tie rewards to good performance. Performance rewards are frequently called incentives. As a rule, they differ from bonuses which are traditionally the perogative of management and are in the form of cash. Incentives are usually something of value, but not always cash. They are short-term reward programs and manifest themselves in a variety of ways, from simple recognition programs to expensive travel rewards. They key to incentives is to reward the appropriate behavior.

A facility is well on its way to providing quality service when its conscious competents have been properly educated, trained, coached, and evaluated. However, more is needed. Facility service also depends on a facility's service system.

4
Service Delivery

Empathy: A Critical Service Factor

Caring behavior is what counts in the food-service industry. As previously discussed, it has its roots in the personnel selection process. It must be modeled by management and reflected throughout the organization.

Employees can learn to anticipate what guests want through "role play" carried out during their training. For example, a restaurateur may want the crew to be more attentive to guests who arrive at the restaurant near closing time. Employees can assume roles in a scene in which guests are being seated by a host five minutes before closing. They can thus evoke an experience of being served by people who would rather do their "side work" and go home than service a guests' needs. Role playing helps employees experience a guest's frustration in ordering from a kitchen that is in the process of being shut down.

Since most guests' service needs are basic, they can be anticipated. Guests appreciate being greeted and waited on when they enter an establishment. At the very least, they want to be acknowledged soon after they sit down or step up to a counter. Other guests' needs, such as those stemming from psychological and cultural factors, are more complex and harder to pinpoint. Not everyone understands the concern a mother of three small children has in waiting for food to be delivered from the time of order. What is a reasonable waiting time for an adult is an eternity to a hungry three-year-old.

Guests have high expectations for both courtesy and overall service. Guests' courtesy and service expectations fall into five categories (*15*):

- *Efficiency.* Guests expect speed and the filling of requests accurately despite any difficulties an operation may be having at a particular time.

- *Timeliness.* Guests want convenient operating hours, quick service, and appropriate delivery. How guests perceive timing is what counts. Quick service of an entrée immediately after the appetizer is finished may be desirable to some guests, but annoying to those who want to relax between courses.

- *Handling requests.* Guests assume managers and appropriate staff will handle special requests quickly and effectively. When their requests cannot be accommodated, guests expect to be informed and given a plausible explanation.

- *Friendly Staff.* Guests expect employees to have positive behavior, be knowledgeable about products and services, and be helpful.

- *Managers and supervisors.* Guests prefer that managers have a pleasing appearance and are visible to them during service times. Guests appreciate when managers have positive attitudes and are available for guest interaction and feedback.

To ensure meeting these service expectations, an emphasis on anticipating guests' needs should be included in guest service training and reinforced through supervision and "shopper" service.

Engineering

Engineering is another critical factor in giving service. It involves systematically designing and planning all service tasks so that crews can spend their time attending to guests' needs. This includes the optimum use of available resources in layout and design, equipment and capital, and in order taking and delivery procedures. Engineering service is based on the ability of managers to:

- *Understand the service system as a system.* They must know the entire guest ordering/delivery needs and wants from point of entry to leaving. They should evaluate each service activity to ascertain the strengths and weaknesses of it in relationship to the guests' needs.

- *Recognize new foodservice production technologies that expedite service.* Included are the computerized point-of-sale registers, conveyor ovens, and audio ordering.

- *Anticipate change.* Managers must attempt to envision future guest needs, service demands, and possible technology. While forecasts are never entirely accurate, change is inevitable. Managers must anticipate what menu items, service systems, and facility features will change. There is no such thing as a perfect restaurant design over any extended period. This is illustrated by the great number of fast-service restaurants built in the 1960s and 1970s with no room for drive-through service.

- *Set goals and objectives.* This gives managers standards for measuring accomplishments. Written goals and objectives also help clarify the company's direction and communicate it to all employees.

- *Identify tasks to be done.* Once goals and objectives are set, they can be divided into separate tasks. These tasks are then evaluated according to employee capabilities.

- *Estimate the costs.* This includes real costs (such as increased labor expenses) for a specific change in service delivery, and intangible costs (such as inconvenience to the staff).

- *Organize and adjust service activities.* Managers group tasks into jobs, assign responsibilities for those jobs, and acquire and assign necessary resources (personnel, equipment, space, and so forth) (*2*).

The Facilities

When facilities are not properly engineered, it makes quality service difficult to achieve. Attending to the entire establishment including outside areas, special rooms, and restrooms is an important, although frequently overlooked, aspect of providing guest service. Following are guidelines for engineering restaurant components that are critical to quality service.

Outside Areas

The outside of a facility reflects the service provided inside. Well-lighted, carefully maintained grounds, including lawns, parking areas, and walkways, are inviting to guests and make them feel secure. Maintaining grounds includes keeping grass and shrubs trimmed, ensuring that walkways are clear of obstacles, ice, and snow, and using bug lights and repellents when necessary.

Guests appreciate when parking areas are convenient to the facility's entrance and the way to the entrance is clearly marked. If valet parking is offered, guests need to feel assured that their automobiles will be driven carefully and be protected from harm, and that car keys will be kept in a secure location. If guests need to wait outdoors for attendants to bring their cars, there should be a sheltered area to protect them from inclement weather. Charges for parking and tipping policies should be posted.

Outdoor dining areas require special attention. They must be:

- *Accessible.* Paths leading to them should be obvious and barrier free. Ground surfaces should not be slippery or damaging to guests' shoes.

- *Protected from strong winds and other harsh climatic factors.* Guests enjoy a breeze, but do not appreciate when their food and utensils won't stay on the table.

- *Constantly monitored and cleaned.* Dust, soot, and debris collect quickly on outdoor equipment. Guests need to feel assured that their clothing will remain clean.

- *Serviced with the same level of service as tables inside the facility.* Systems are needed that ensure effective service delivery to outdoor dining areas even though they may be farther from the kitchen than indoor areas. Guests sitting outside feel freer to leave an establishment if there is no server in sight.

Coat Checks

Coat rooms are typically located near entrances. For guests' comfort, the areas near coat rooms should be heated and free from drafts. Guests expect coat check systems to ensure the speedy and efficient taking in and delivery of their belongings even during peak business hours. Signs are needed to state policies concerning acceptance of fur coats, coat checking charges, and tipping policies. Coat checkers provide guest service when they are courteous and conscientious. More effective service can be provided when coat check and valet services are coordinated.

Waiting Areas

Most guests do not enjoy waiting for a table, so restaurateurs must make the wait as bearable as possible. Guests become irate when they suspect other guests are receiving preferential treatment in being seated. It is critical that employees adhere to the name or numbering system used to seat guests.

Waiting areas with comfortable seating are always appreciated. Hosts and hostesses need to check these areas frequently, so guests do not feel ignored. When paging systems are used, they should be audible, but not overly loud and disruptive to those dining in the facility. When bars are used as waiting areas, alternative space should be provided for guests who are not comfortable in bars. Having some type of guest distraction makes waiting seem shorter. Providing menus for guests to read or offering complimentary treats are value-added extras that make waiting more pleasant (this is discussed more fully in Chapter 5).

Smoking and Non-smoking Sections

Some states and municipalities have enacted legislation regarding restaurant seating and smoking. Restrictions on smoking sections vary. In Aspen, Colorado, smoking is prohibited in restaurants except in separate rooms equipped with ventilation systems. Other states or municipalities require restaurants to set aside a percentage of seating for non-smoking sections. Many restaurateurs are opposed to such ordinances. They claim:

- "Antismoking ordinances impose unreasonable costs on private businesses, costs that are passed on to the consuming public in the form of higher-priced goods and services" (7).

- Servers offend guests when they are required to ask them to refrain from smoking. "Customers want friendly, efficient waiters and waitresses, not non-smoking hall monitors" (7).

- Restaurants lose business because people are unwilling to wait to be seated in the section of their choice.

Proponents of the ordinances cite Gallup research indicating that only 35 percent of the adult population smokes, and that when restaurants are equally divided into smoking and non-smoking sections, guests are more likely to have to wait for seating in the non-smoking section. As one restaurateur wrote, "We have our restaurant equally divided into both smoking and non-smoking sections. Upon entering our restaurant, each guest is asked which section he or she prefers. We have never taken a rigid poll, but I will honestly wager that 65 percent of my total guest count sits in the non-smoking section" (9).

Those favoring the legislation also cite that "Customers are increasingly naming cigarette smoke as one of the most disturbing elements of dining out" (4). Gallup research shows that 36 percent of respondents would not return to a restaurant because it did not have a non-smoking section (14). As one restaurant guest states, "Sure, non-smoking areas cost money, so do clean restrooms, quality food, and pest control ... I recall with tears in my eyes the times my expensive dinner was ruined by smoke from those near me, people who in many cases had already enjoyed theirs" (9).

When non-smoking sections are introduced to restaurants, management, not guests, have the enforcement responsibility.

Restrooms

Clean, well-stocked restrooms convey to guests that their comforts are important to the restaurant. Restrooms that are not clean, sanitary, and odor-free are unacceptable. In addition to cleaning restrooms regularly during off-peak hours and monitoring them during busy periods, the checklist in Chart 4.1 lists how operators can provide better hospitality and increase guest comfort.

Telephone Areas

Guests expect access to a public telephone in a restaurant. It is considered a guest convenience. A checklist for providing guest service in the telephone area is given in Chart 4.2.

Private Rooms

Many restaurants have separate rooms or areas for private functions. They range from the simple to the elaborate in decor and services. Guests may select food from the regular menu, there may be a separate menu for private functions, or guests may use the regular menu as a base and add special items. One restaurant offers custom-designed meals in its private rooms and special amenities. "Some of the room

---

Chart 4.1. Restroom Service Checklist

— *Signs clearly identify restrooms.* While a silhouette of a man or woman is an attractive alternative to "Men" and "Women" signs, these pictures must obviously indicate which room is for whom—very abstract representations can confuse guests.

— *Restrooms are well-lighted and in good repair.* Broken tiles, out-of-order plumbing, and nonworking soap dispensers and towel dryers are guest inconveniences.

— *Facilities comply with barrier-free requirements for disabled guests and extra considerations are provided.* Disabled guests appreciate equipment and supplies that are accessible to them and easy to operate.

— *Rooms are spotless and properly maintained.* Sinks, floors, walls, ceilings, stalls, and toilets shine. Stall locks are intact. The plumbing is perfect. Trash pails and sanitary bins are emptied regularly and never allowed to overflow. When there are unavoidable equipment breakdowns, legible "out-of-order" signs are posted.

— *Stalls are adequate in size, have well-placed paper holders, convenience hooks, and pull-down shelves.*

— *Supplies are adequate.* Toilet paper, soap, and paper towels (if used) are always available. When extra supplies such as toilet seat covers are provided, they also are restocked as necessary.

— *Sink areas are designed with guests in mind.* Hot and cold water taps are clearly designated. When guests are using sinks, the soap dispensers, method of hand-drying, and trash containers are within reach. Soap dispensers are full, unclogged, and clean. Hot air dryers are operational, the air is directed downward away from guests' faces, and the air is the proper temperature. Trash containers are of sufficient size to accommodate the garbage that accumulates until the next scheduled emptying.

— *There is a grooming area separate from the sink area.* This provides adequate room for grooming activities and also helps prevent sinks from getting clogged with hair.

— *Vending machines are operational and stocked.* This is especially necessary for machines that dispense women's sanitary supplies.

— *Children's needs are met.* Guests with infants and toddlers require diaper changing areas. Those with older children appreciate equipment (sinks, toilets, and drinking fountains) their children can reach.

— *Attendants are properly groomed and trained.* Tipping policies are clearly stated.

Chart 4.1. Restroom Service Checklist (continued)

— *Seating (chairs or couches) are provided.* These are useful for guests who need to rest briefly or who are not feeling well.

— *There are extras.* Some restaurants provide complimentary extras, such as deodorant sprays, perfumes and colognes, and single-use disposable products such as toothbrushes, combs, and soap packets. Other guest extras include safety pins, needles, and thread.

Chart 4.2. Telephone Area Service Checklist

— *Telephones are located appropriately.* They are in well-lighted, private areas away from noise and guest or employee traffic. Telephones located outside on the grounds of the facility also require adequate lighting and should be away from traffic noises for optimum guest convenience. Guests appreciate when outdoor telephones are sheltered as well. Signs that do not detract from the ambiance of the restaurant inform guests where telephones can be found. Telephones on tables do not take up needed service space.

— *Equipment is clean, sanitary, and functioning.* Worn or broken equipment is promptly replaced.

— *The restaurant's telephone numbers are visible.* The telephone number of the instrument being used as well as the telephone number of the restaurant are posted. Guests frequently have to tell others where they can be reached.

— *Change is available.* Guests of the facility can get change for telephone calls upon request. Some facilities provide change machines.

— *A telephone directory is provided.* The directory is near the telephone and is complete. Some facilities use protective covers to cut down on wear, as well as devices to secure the directories so they cannot be removed. Even when a directory is secured, it should still be convenient to use and monitored for worn or missing pages.

— *Added-value services.* Guests appreciate when a pen or pencil and note paper to write down telephone numbers or messages are available in the telephone area, and they like to have a place to sit and converse in privacy.

amenities are a private elevator, valet parking in the building, a movable parquet dance floor, a baby grand piano, a dressing room, a reception foyer, and optional limousine service. In planning the menu, clients who are undecided about what to order are invited to private tastings" (*6*).

Three areas of service design in private rooms are frequently overlooked: 1) An efficient means for getting the food to the function room; 2) food and equipment holding and storage areas; and 3) appropriate guest parking (it is possible to fill a restaurant's parking lot with guest automobiles and present an image of being extremely busy in the dining room when in reality no guests are there).

To provide outstanding service to guests in private rooms, facilities:

- *Ensure that private rooms are well-located.* Guests require access to coat check rooms, telephones, and restrooms. Some restaurants have separate facilities for private functions. Many ensure that private rooms are very convenient to the kitchen.

- *Arrange and set up tables in advance.* This ensures efficient service, especially when all details, including place cards, centerpieces, and special instructions, have been attended to.

- *Provide adequate staffing.* The level of service at a private function is as important as it is in public dining areas.

- *Have sufficient room so that business can be conducted or entertainment can be provided.* Meetings frequently entail special equipment. Special occasions are often celebrated with entertainment, such as music or dancing.

- *Provide guests with necessary information.* Contracts regarding fees and services for private rooms help avoid communications problems between restaurateurs and guests. These typically include information concerning date, time, number of people expected, and cancellation policy; services provided; description of the menu; costs; what constitutes extras; guests' special requests; and restaurant policies, such as whether or not a guest can decorate a room.

Delivery Systems and Their Components

A delivery system is the process used to deliver products and services to guests. Systems may vary according to facility type and service style but they all require engineering. Following are basic types of delivery systems used in restaurants today, along with some of their structural procedures:

- *Restaurant table service.* The variations of restaurant table service include:

  French service. French service is most often found in higher-priced, sophisticated establishments. In French service, unprepared or partially-prepared food is arranged and garnished on platters in the kitchen. Servers bring the platters to tables for guest approval. Then, much of the preparation, finishing, or carving of the food is done on a cart in front of the guest. French service is labor-intensive. It requires extra service personnel with culinary knowledge and skills and, frequently, added employees to wash the extra dishes involved. Increased costs also result because the facility must have adequate space to accommodate the carts and food preparation, special equipment is required and typically, there is a slower turnover of tables.

  Russian service. This is similar to French service, except carving and finishing are completed in the kitchen. The finished dishes are arranged on trays, garnished, and presented to guests for inspection. Servers then place the food on empty plates already set before the guests. Although common in Europe, this type of service is rarely found in the United States. It is an elegant service style and contributes to a quality image.

  American service. When American service is used, all food is placed on plates and garnished in the kitchen. Servers then place a plate in front of each guest. American service is used widely today because it is quick and requires less staff.

  English service. This service style is primarily used at celebrations where there is a host or hostess. Food is brought to them for apportioning or serving to their guests. For example, a host or hostess may carve meat or slice a birthday cake and then either serve the other guests themselves or have a server do so.

  Family-style service. In family-style service, the food is brought to the table on platters and in bowls (which helps save time in the kitchen), and guests serve themselves. Some control over portioning is lost because guests at the table determine the size of their own portions.

  Self-service. Guests help themselves with varying amounts of assistance from production personnel, depending on the style of facility.

Many restaurateurs use a combination of these service styles. Soup may be served and garnished in the kitchen, guests may help themselves to salad from a salad bar, the entrée may be brought in on a platter, and the dessert may be prepared on a cart at tableside or served by a host or hostess.

Service also can be classified according to how food is brought to the customer: arm service, tray service, or cart service:

> *Arm service.* This type of service is mostly used in very casual facilities, such as diners or coffee shops. Servers carry individual plates of food from the kitchen to the guest.

> *Tray service.* This is most often used with American service. A large tray is used to carry plates filled with food to a stand in the dining area in the vicinity of the guests. Servers then carry the plates to the guests' tables.

> *Cart service.* In cart service (often used in French service), servers use a rolling cart to transport food to the guest table area for finishing.

Table Service and HOT Spots

There are critical Hospitality Opportunity Times—HOT spots pertaining to table service (*3*):

• *Appropriate greeting and seating.* The seating of the guests is of vital importance to guest satisfaction. Under extreme conditions when guests have been standing in line, it is usual policy to seat a guest at the first available table of appropriate size. However, in most cases, guests should be seated according to their needs or preferences. Dining rooms are usually designed to accommodate a number of different party sizes and guest preferences through their layout, design, lighting, sound, and table size. Some guest service ideas to consider include:

Privacy in public. Private areas are designed for people who wish to dine in relative seclusion. They frequently are high-back booth seats, are in corners, or are next to walls. One designer created a private room out of what would have been a most unpleasant space near the kitchen entrance. It became sought after by small groups who wanted to dine in privacy. Another designed large chairs with 48-inch backs to create private space in the center of the dining room.

The business space. This space has many of the benefits of the privacy in public space; however, it addresses other needs of business meals. Some of these special considerations are controlled lighting (rheostats), phone jacks, sound control to mask discussions, and the availability of writing materials. Individualized small meeting rooms are most appropriate to encourage business meal patronage.

Center stage. Center stage is an area which allows people to see and be seen. When designing this space, it is important to understand the facility's market. Center stage is also popular in lounge areas for guests who are celebrating.

The view. Some restaurants have the advantage of a view. This provides guests with a unique experience and is often especially enjoyed by tourists and "occasion" diners. A restaurant with a view should be designed so as many guests as possible can enjoy it. Abundant glass and tiered seating are two popular approaches.

The naturally bright spot. Many people enjoy the naturally-lighted space which is commonly provided today by skylights or glass enclosures such as greenhouses.

There are certain spaces in dining rooms that are less desirable than others. Most often these include seating near entrances, near kitchens, close to high traffic areas, and tight uncomfortable spaces. Consideration should be given in layout and design to anticipate these conditions, so that partitions and other reliefs can be used to create more desirable seating spaces.

Anticipation of needs. An empathetic and experienced host often anticipates a party's needs before being asked. It is a matter of observing the non-verbal symbols. For example, when guests come in for lunch dressed in business attire, carrying briefcases, and seriously conversing, they will more than likely want to discuss business. They will require a table in a quiet corner away from a group celebrating a child's birthday. Whenever any doubt exists about the meal occasion, the guests should be asked what their preferences are. Avoid saying "no." When guests' requests cannot be met because of lack of product or staff, a specific area is closed, or tables are reserved, seaters must approach all service requests from the perspective of how the guests' needs can be satisfied. When offering an alternative or before denying a request, they must be tactful and seat guests intelligently. Guests resent being crowded at adjoining tables or being offered the least desirable table when a restaurant is not full. Quality service may be placing a party of two at a table for four when space permits. Consideration must be provided all parties, and when seating children, older guests, the disabled, or people with other special needs, extra considerations may be required.

- *One-minute attention.* After guests have been seated, they should be attended to as quickly as possible. (An attention standard of one to three minutes frequently is used.) Table attention refers to any form of acknowledgement that signifies service has begun. Although it may not always be possible to actually provide service within the standard, guests must feel assured that service personnel are aware of their presence and that they will be attended to shortly. This activity can include bus service of water, bread, butter, or some other "instant food." At times, it may consist of nothing more than body language, a facial expression, or a signal from the service person that indicates, "I see you there, I'm rushed at the moment, but I'll be there shortly." Professionals can communicate this message in a split second.

- *Menu presentation.* Traditional industry practice has been for either seaters or servers to provide guests with menus at the time of seating. This practice should also be followed for guests who have been having cocktails while waiting for tables. However, this procedure may not always be appropriate, particularly in restaurants where beverages are merchandised. Frequently, it is wiser to first present guests with the beverage and appetizer menus. When there are no written menus or when there are unlisted specials, servers recite what is available. Care should be taken that the number of unlisted specials does not bewilder guests. Most guests will be somewhat confused when more than three items are recited at one time. If an unusual service procedure is used in the facility, such as buffet-style service, salad bars, or dessert tables, guests should be informed when they are seated.

- *Cocktail service.* When restaurants serve cocktails, servers or seaters (depending on company policy) approach the table shortly after guests are seated. The guests are greeted and asked if they are ready to order cocktails. Cocktail orders typically are taken in sequence around the table using a numbering (or other) system so that the drinks, when served, can be matched to the guests who ordered them.

    "The simplest system is to establish one point in the room, such as the door, as a starting base. All seats facing the point are designated as [seat] 1, with the other seats numbered consecutively, clockwise around the table. If the guests at seats . . . 2 and . . . 4 are . . . [female] their orders may be taken first, but be designated according to their seats. In this way, the party can served their orders properly, without . . . [servers] having to keep a number of orders in . . . [their heads] or to interrupt the guests' conversation with questions" (3). This system is also used to enable any server to pick up and serve another employee's table.

Guests' preferences for premium or special brands are noted and guests are informed when these items are unavailable (remember, good service is never having to say no). Servers then place the cocktail order at the bar and obtain and serve the cocktails. Effective servers keep a sharp eye on the table for cues that guests either want a second round of drinks or are ready to order. Servers have to sense how to pace a guest's service. (Servers do have to take care that if they are conversing with one another and watching for cues from the guests at the same time, they don't appear to be talking about the guests. When conversing, the tendency is for the servers to whisper and keep shifting their eyes to the guest thus creating that impression.)

- *Food order taking.* Determining the exact moment when guests are ready to order is a learned skill. Some guests may need only to glance at the menu, while others like to study it or discuss selections with servers or others in their party. Usually, the signal of guests closing their menus indicates that they are ready to order.

  Traditionally, orders are taken from children and female guests first. Many servers use a numbering system (such as that described under cocktails) to keep track of who ordered what, and to avoid the discourteous practice of "auctioning" off each dish when it is served.

- *Wine orders.* Wine orders are taken immediately following food orders according to most restaurants' policies. This allows the wine selection to be made to complement foods and guests' preferences. Servers should know their wine lists and be prepared to recommend an appropriate wine at a guest's request.

- *Instant food and drink stimulators.* Accompaniments such as bread, butter, water, tortilla chips, salsa, relish trays, or other items are often provided guests immediately after they are seated. This practice has several advantages: 1) it encourages beverage sales; 2) provides guests with something to neutralize their hunger; and 3) reduces the guest's perception of slow service during peak periods. These items may be placed on the table before the guests order their pre-meal beverages. At this time, servers also double-check that all necessary linens, flatware, and serviceware are on the table and provide any missing items.

- *Placing orders and obtaining them from the kitchen.* Transmitting food orders to the kitchen quickly and accurately is a key component of good service. A clearly written or entered order prevents errors that cause guest dissatisfaction. Servers need to know the preparation times involved in handling special requests, in order to coordinate service delivery to a table.

- *Hot foods hot and cold foods cold.* One research study indicates that when guests define quality foodservice, the two words most used to describe quality food are *taste* and *hot.* Thus, servers must ensure that hot foods are served hot, and cold foods are served cold by being alert to when their orders are ready. Some facilities use paging or light systems for this purpose. Typically, cold items are picked up before hot items and placed on the service tray. When loaded, the service tray should contain all necessary items and be balanced to avoid accidents.

- *The expeditor system.* A frequently used effective food delivery system employs "delivery expeditors" or "food runners." These assistant service personnel deliver food from the kitchen to the appropriate dining room station. They do not serve the food (this is the responsibility of the service personnel), but they do return soiled dishes and serviceware to the kitchen.

- *Appetizers are served after or during beverage service.* Before serving appetizers, servers remove all used dishes and empty cocktail glasses from the table, taking care that guests are truly finished with their drinks.

- *Soups and / or salads are served after cocktail service.* If soups have been ordered as appetizers, it is appropriate to ask guests if they would like their soup and salad served at the same or different time. When guests have finished eating their appetizers, soups, or salads, all used dishes and utensils are removed and the server again checks to ensure that all required linen, flatware, and serviceware are on the table and replaces what is missing.

- *Entrées are served.* After the party has begun to eat, the server returns to the table within minutes to see that all is acceptable. Any problems or complaints must be reported to appropriate managerial personnel and satisfaction delivered immediately (see how to handle a complaint in Chapter 6 of this text).

- *Completed entrées.* When guests have completed their entrees, all plates and soiled utensils are removed from the table and the table or cloth is cleaned.

- *The dessert or after-dinner beverage.* Following table clearing, the dessert order is taken. Dessert merchandising is a developed skill. Dessert is ordered more frequently when servers display the desserts on trays and carts and use suggestion techniques ("Can I get you some fabulous Bavarian chocolate mousse or a piece of our strawberry cheesecake a la rum?" rather than "Do you want any dessert?"). Coffee, tea, and other after-dinner beverage orders are also taken and filled at this point.

- *The manager visits.* At least once during the meal, the manager should take the opportunity to visit the table and provide personal attention. However, there are occasions when visiting a table to converse is inappropriate. But, this is the exception rather than the rule. One restaurant's service policy requires that all parties of five or more must be visited by the manager who delivers some unexpected extra at least once during the meal (usually during the cocktail period).

- *Preparing and presenting the check and collecting payment.* Checks are filled out as completely and accurately as possible when guest orders are taken. "Prechecking" (writing or entering, pricing, and totaling the check before the order is picked up from the kitchen) is standard procedure in many establishments. Typically, taxes are not computed at the ordering point, because additional items, such as dessert, coffee, or after-dinner drinks, may have to be added to the check before the tax can be figured.

  After the host has questioned the guest about the need for any additional service, the guest check is usually presented facedown on the table, on a tray, or in a folder to the guest who has requested it. The check is delivered when the server thanks the guests for coming, asks how they enjoyed their meals, and invites them to come again. If a guest reaches immediately for money or a credit card when the check is delivered, the server waits for the payment and takes it to the cashier. When a guest is not immediately prepared to pay, the server leaves the table but keeps an eye on the party and responds promptly when summoned. Servers return all change to guests and never take for granted that the change is a gratuity.

- *Clearing the table and resetting for subsequent guests.* Immediately after guests have left, tables are cleared and reset for the next guests. Clearing and resetting quickly keeps the dining room looking attractive for guests who are entering and provides a more appealing environment for guests who are already dining nearby.

  Cleared dishes and utensils are neatly and securely stacked according to the restaurant's warewashing procedures. They are removed from the dining area as quickly as possible, along with all table scraps. Guests do not want to see the remnants of their meals or those of other guests.

  Soiled tablecloths are always replaced. To minimize offending guests, a tablecloth can be changed by folding back the cloth halfway and placing the clean cloth over the exposed section of the table. Then, the soiled cloth is folded back as the clean cloth is unfolded into position.

  When resetting the table, water glasses and cups are sometimes placed upside down to prevent them from collecting dust.

Fast-Service

An efficient delivery system carried out by hospitable employees is the primary element in successful fast-service restaurants. A fast-service system is designed to provide consistent-quality, familiar foods fast, and at moderate to inexpensive prices. Fast-service has mass market appeal. Because of the emphasis on quickness and efficiency, the fast-service delivery system is dependent on mass production technology, task specialization, and the division of labor to serve guests faster and better. A typical fast-service restaurant has several different employee work centers, including the cashier/host, grill, fry station, and "make-up" and packing areas, as well as storage and housekeeping areas.

The cashier/host area must be viewed as the guest service station in fast-service restaurants. In many fast-service establishments, employees rotate among the work centers, necessitating that they learn a variety of tasks. This concept of rotation is effective if managers ensure that all employees who come in contact with guest have guest service qualifications and training.

While most fast-service functions occur just as in table service, guests' labor replaces many of the full-service host's duties.

- *Instant guest greeting.* The pivotal position for hospitable service in a fast-service restaurant is held by guest contact personnel. They have literally seconds to take orders, suggestively sell, and establish the relationship of hospitality. These are the same people who are the most effective in production and all too often are not assigned guest contact duties. The counter person is responsible for making guests feel welcome, taking and expediting their order, and cashiering. These employees are the company's representatives and must be fast, courteous, and responsive to guests even at peak service times. The key to communicating hospitality at this service point includes the ability to be friendly and efficient (which is sometimes in conflict under stress). Counter people require the ability to make eye contact, smile quickly, make an appropriate salutation, and have a regard for guests as individuals in order to assess their particular needs.

- *Order taking.* After a guest approaches the counter, the order is taken promptly. But, guests who are reading the menu board should not be rushed or intimidated.

- *Suggestive selling.* After guests request their initial order, counter person/cashiers can make appropriate suggestions to increase sales. For example, a counter person/cashier may suggest to a parent that a family-pack of chicken might be more convenient and economical than ordering three separate dinners. Guests appreciate suggestions when they are offered in a friendly, descriptive, non-demanding manner, and when they feel they will benefit from the advice.

- *Order verification.* After guests place their orders, counter person/cashiers recite them so guests can verify their accuracy.

- *Accepting payment.* In most fast-service units, guests pay before their orders are filled to ensure that counter personnel remember to collect payment. Counter personnel inform guests of the total in a clear voice. The money received by the employee is placed on the shelf of the cash register until after the change has been accepted by the guest. Change is counted aloud. Only when the guest is satisfied with the correct change, is the money placed in the cash register drawer.

- *Filling the order.* In many fast-service restaurants (or during peak hours at others) there are back-up counter personnel who do not deal directly with customers, but are responsible for filling orders. In other establishments, counter personnel fill orders themselves. Counter employees work most efficiently when prepared food dispensers are properly stocked. Counter people who must wait for unavailable products, prepare their own drinks, or have inadequate change in their registers cannot provide efficient service. Of course, equipment breakdowns, personnel shortages, and poor facility design also hamper guest service.

Food is prepared by production personnel who ensure that there is an optimum amount on hand to fill orders. Keeping up with demand during busy periods is probably the most difficult aspect of their jobs. Production personnel require the cooperation of counter personnel to perform efficiently. They need to be properly and clearly informed of special requests and large orders. They also perform better when all equipment functions properly, working conditions are adequate, and products and supplies are conveniently situated.

Counter personnel place completed orders on serving trays or in bags or boxes depending on the guests' preferences and include all necessary condiments, straws, or other items according to restaurant policy. For take-out, hot and cold items are generally separated when packaged. Employees double-check to ensure that every item ordered has been included. Then, counter personnel hand orders to guests with a smile and a "thank you."

Service Standards

Fast-service restaurants regularly measure guest serving time (GST) by monitoring guests from the time they complete their order until they receive their food. The aim of most establishments is to cut the GST to a minimum, while still providing friendly guest service. When standard times have been established by managers, crews frequently are able to improve upon these standards.

Upgraded Dining Room Service in Fast-Service Restaurants

Since the size of dining rooms in many fast-service restaurants has been increasing, more attention is being given to upgrading guest service activities. To facilitate upgraded service, some operations are taking the following steps:

- Managers are remaining in the dining room during peak sales periods. They visit tables, interact with guests, offer refills, and help out as necessary with other tasks.

- Hosts are being posted at entrances.
- Personnel are assigned to clear and clean tables.
- Televisions are installed in dining rooms.
- Free refills on beverages are offered.
- There is table delivery of food.

Drive-Through Service

Drive-through systems are most often found in the fast-service segment of the industry. As the ultimate in guest convenience, many drive-through units are designed to offer food in less than one minute from guest order to pick up.

According to industry reports, drive-through windows make up as much as 50 percent of total sales in many fast-service chains and that number is growing. "It's no secret that as fast-[service] chains battle market saturation and customers demand convenience, drive-through service will continue to gain momentum. Many restaurants now feature two-window service instead of one for handling peak volumes; the first window is for collection, the second for product delivery. Cost-effective drive-through-only units have surfaced in space-starved regions" (13).

In a typical drive-through operation, guests order food by talking to employees through a speaker located near a menu board outside the restaurant. The employee listens to the order and fills it in much the same way as is done with inside service. Guests then drive to a pick-up window to pay for and pick up their orders or, in some operations, guests order and pay for their food at one window station and drive to another for pick up.

Drive-through guests are sometimes offered a more limited menu than those who walk in, but the delivery system for both is similar. However, because drive-through customers are waiting in cars and traffic tends to back up at peak hours, the quickest service possible becomes even more important. Also, special packaging of drive-through orders is critical. Since guests must drive with the food in their cars, even if just to the other end of the parking area, spill-proof, leak-proof food containers are required.

There are many innovations which are helping restaurants provide more efficient drive-through service, including:

- The construction of drive-through-only mobile units that are designed to provide fast and efficient service in very small areas.

- A wireless headset that enables clear, quality communication between guests and employees who are located at any point inside the facility. This eliminates the need for an employee to stay at the drive-through window during slow times and enables employees to take drive-through orders from anywhere in the restaurant.

- Automated sliding windows in drive-through units enable employees to hand out packages without manually operating the window. Their hands are free to take money and assist the guest with the package. These windows have cut service time 20 percent at one company (*10*).

Cafeteria Service

Cafeterias offer efficient food delivery based on the customer's participation in the process. However, many industry experts regard the cafeteria's delivery system as more complex than other types of operations. "There is no single more efficient way to feed people than a cafeteria. But it is labor intensive. The biggest problem is finding the right number of employees. You need 30 to 50 employees to open a cafeteria . . . They have to learn how to carve, how to bake, to cook, [and how] to cut pies. In fast-[service], you're responsible for maybe 15 or 18 items. At a cafeteria . . . there can be as many as . . . 500" (*8*).

The future looks excellent for cafeteria service. Besides appreciating their efficiency, many guests prefer the range of foods cafeterias offer. As one industry analyst explains, "Cafeterias are less vulnerable to recessional influences than are other restaurant concepts. One reason is the price/value perception, the key selling point for a cafeteria. Most chains average about $4 per check, not much higher than a fast-food outlet and with considerably more variety on the menu" (*8*).

Cafeteria guests have the added advantage of being able to control the pace of food delivery. They can move quickly through the cafeteria line or linger over their selections. They enjoy selecting from appetizing displays and like the idea that self-service often eliminates the need for a gratuity.

But, like all other foodservice operations, cafeterias require careful staffing and attention to run efficiently. There must be enough employees on duty to keep the cafeteria's food selection fresh and fully stocked. Guests find picked over or dried out menu offerings offensive, and resent when their favorite foods are unavailable. They want their foods well-prepared and at the right temperatures.

Sanitation is vital in cafeterias. All tongs, ladles, dispensers, and other serving utensils used should be cleaned and replaced frequently in accordance with local health codes. This procedure should be adhered to whether food is served by employees or is selected by guests.

Cafeteria delivery systems are designed so that guests can pick up trays, rest them on a bar or shelf, and move quickly and smoothly through a defined selection path. Guests pay cashiers who are usually positioned at the end of the path.

Traditionally, guests move in a single line through a cafeteria; however, the newest trend in cafeteria delivery systems is the use of several scattered foodservice stations instead of a single line.

Cashiers need to be friendly and courteous and remind guests to pick up needed utensils, napkins, or condiments at designated areas. At both the cashier and utensil areas, guests require enough space to set down their trays while they pay or select items.

In a cafeteria, many guests pitch in and clean up when there are adequate, visible trash containers positioned conveniently around the room. These containers are emptied frequently by housekeeping personnel to make it easy for guests to dispose of unsightly trash and to avoid odor problems. Clean-up employees are on hand at all times to clear tables, clean tables and chairs, mop up spills, and remove trash. A manager, or other employee, is usually available in the dining area to greet guests, answer questions, offer help to those guests who require it, take complaints, and resolve problems.

Off-Premises Delivery

Designing a quality system for home delivery is perhaps the most challenging of all service delivery systems. Operators must deliver quality products to guests in a minimum amount of time and deal with a variety of unforeseen factors along the way. In addition to extra kitchen organization, home or office delivery requires competent drivers, transportation that ensures food will keep its quality, accurate and limited delivery routes, and extra liability insurance. To protect product quality, some restaurants have delivery vehicles containing ovens and refrigeration equipment so proper food temperatures can be maintained. They also are using insulated containers to package products.

In a typical operation, when the order is called in, an employee answers the telephone by identifying the restaurant in a clear and courteous manner. The employee requests the caller's name, address, and telephone number, writes down the information, and repeats it for verification.

The order is taken and is transmitted at once to the kitchen. The employee usually provides the guest with an estimated delivery time. The food order is filled by production personnel and packed using special containers or wraps. These ensure that guests receive intact, ready-to-eat products. Order checks are affixed to the packaging, frequently along with a menu to promote repeat business.

Guest service depends on the deliverer's ability to move the food quickly from the restaurant to the customer. Those who deliver need to be knowledgeable about possible delivery routes and be prepared to take alternate roads when there are tie-ups. Since it is the delivery person who serves as the company representative in this service style, this employee must be presentable and friendly. Delivery personnel collect payment from guests, professionally present them with the food, and thank them.

Innovations to improve off-premises service delivery include:

- *Dedicated management and crew.* One of the critical elements of successful off-premises delivery is to recognize that it is a specialized business which should be managed and marketed separately from other restaurant services.

- *Historical guest information.* This is displayed on the facility's computer terminal and is useful for building relationships between the restaurant and guest. It can be the basis for suggestive selling, target recall, or be used in conjunction with other marketing tools.

- *Computerized ordering systems.* These enable the order to be transmitted electronically from the guest's telephone to the restaurant via a central processing area.

- *Mobile units.* These are used so food can be inventoried or prepared en route to the guest (5).

- *Tiny, three-wheeled vehicles.* These units are especially designed for food delivery and can go as far as 80 miles on one gallon of gasoline (11).

Systems That Work

There are many success stories in the area of service management, but some of the most impressive are the service systems that have been developed by the fast-service industry.

The goal of many productivity models is to motivate employees to increase guest satisfaction by decreasing service time. Typically, employees identify barriers and problems in the service system. Then, they are encouraged to offer solutions. Group discussions are used to motivate employees to become involved with improving productivity. Solutions are then implemented. Finally, productivity models are evaluated by comparing serving times before and after implementation. Managers and employee groups determine if the productivity plan is as effective as expected and changes are instituted as necessary. Restaurants that encourage employee input build an enthusiastic team of employees who stay on longer, reduce guest serving time, decrease the amount of employee labor, and increase the dollars per hour taken in by counter personnel.

Measuring results is the only true way to determine the effectiveness of service systems. Traditional methods of measuring results include studying sales figures by preparing a profit-and-loss statement and analyzing guest counts and transactions.

A profit-and-loss (P&L) statement is a summary of the business income and expense transactions for a specific period. It includes items such as net sales, cost of goods sold, payroll and related expenses, direct operating expenses, operating profit, and profit (or loss) before taxes (1). Also called an earnings statement, income statement, or operating statement, the profit-and-loss statement provides managers with valuable information that helps them compare current performance against past performance, plan future business strategy, project future operating income and expenses, and make day-to-day operating decisions. A sample restaurant profit-and-loss statement appears in Chart 4.3.

Many managers use comparative profit-and-loss statements to determine whether new service programs and procedures are efficient and effective. This comes as no surprise since business is most often "bottom line" driven.

The profit-and-loss statement, however, is usually a short term measure of efficiency and focuses on quantitative, not qualitative results. In other words, if a restaurant experiences extreme sales volume increases because the national softball championships were held in its community in a given month, it is more than likely sales would be up and labor costs would be down. But, if the restaurant operated with too few labor hours during that period—the efficiency of productivity would look good on paper, even though service quality standards were not met and many guests left dissatisfied. In this case, the profit-and-loss statement would not be a good means of determining the long range, qualitative effect of low service standards.

Chart 4.3. Sample Restaurant Profit-and-Loss Statement*

For the period ending ————

	Full Menu		Limited Menu		Limited Menu/ No Tableservice		Cafeteria	
	Dollars ($000)	Sales Percent	Dollars ($000)	Sales Percent	Dollars ($000)	Sales Percent	Dollars ($000)	Sales Percent
Sales								
Food Sales	1,458	72.9	1,616	80.8	1,958	97.9	1,850	92.5
Beverage Sales	462	23.1	358	17.9	34	1.7	96	4.8
Other Income	80	4.0	26	1.3	8	0.4	54	2.7
Total Net Sales	2,000	100.0	2,000	100.0	2,000	100.0	2,000	100.0
Cost of Goods Sold (COGS)								
Food	610	30.5	640	32.0	648	32.4	782	39.1
Beverage	134	6.7	100	5.0	6	0.3	30	1.5
Total COGS	744	37.2	740	37.0	654	32.7	812	40.6
Gross Margin (Profit)	1,256	62.8	1,260	63.0	1,346	67.3	1,188	59.4
Operating Expense								
Payroll	550	27.5	492	24.6	500	25.0	514	25.7
Other Expense	522	26.1	508	25.4	558	27.9	454	22.7
Total Op. Expense	1,072	53.6	1,000	50.0	1,058	52.9	968	48.4
Operating Profit	184	9.2	260	13.0	288	14.4	220	11.0

* Numbers given are not meant to represent exact figures for the restaurant industry and are used as rounded examples only. "Additional Income" and "Taxes" are not shown here since the P&L statement represents strictly operating figures.

Labor/Cost Efficiency Ratios

Labor cost efficiency ratios are determined by dividing total labor cost by net sales. These ratios are frequently used in the industry because they are easy to determine, and industry norms are readily available for comparison. Their weakness is that high sales, price increases, and underscheduling of labor hours can result in what would appear to be more favorable service management.

Other Ways to Measure Service Efficiency and Effectiveness

Guest counts are perhaps the best long term way to measure service effectiveness. The number of guests served during a specific period can be compared to the number served during a similar period before service procedures, policies, or systems were changed. Increased guest counts indicate (but do not necessarily prove) that the new systems are or are not more effective. There are many ways to drive up guest counts for short periods of time. The most common are:

- Advertising.
- Discount or value-added promotions.
- Increased use of media.
- Publicity.
- Special promotions and events.

When using guest counts to measure service decisions, it is also important to compare the average guest check and typical promotional programs.

More effective measurement standards include:

- Labor hours to meals served ratios.
- Labor hours per guest transaction (fast-service).
- Labor hours per guest count.

Measuring Service Quality

One of the most effective means of evaluating the quality of service is to ask the ultimate judge—*the guest.* There are several means of monitoring guest opinions of restaurant service. They include:

- *Guest intercept surveys.* Managers use these to measure service quality. Guests are asked to answer questions on their way out of the restaurant. The surveys provide information which can be used as a basis for service decision-making. Guests are asked for their opinions on several of the critical benefits of the restaurant, including the quality of food, service, cleanliness, friendliness, and value-to-price benefit. When a formal survey of a sample of 200 guests per meal period is taken quarterly, it can be determined whether guests' perceptions of services are improving, are less favorable, or are unchanging.

- *Guest comment cards.* These are another way operations measure the effects of management changes in service systems. Since managing service depends on what satisfies guests, guests are in the best position to tell management what works and what does not. Guests are usually quite willing to share their comments both verbally and in writing if they think there is a sincere interest in their opinions and their views will lead to change. Comment cards are frequently placed on tables and a locked suggestion box is provided so that poor service comments cannot be discarded by anyone.

However, the most effective means of quality service control is a caring manager who is "working the floor" observing, talking, and probing for guest comments.

5

Service Extras Count

Unexpected Extras

Value is a perception that cannot be quantitatively measured. It is a feeling guests have when leaving a restaurant that they have received more than their money's worth. There are many elements in a restaurant that contribute to this feeling or perception. Perhaps, the most important one to the mass market is the restaurant's food—its taste, appearance, and quantity relative to price. An obvious element to a great restaurant's success is that guests always leave with their hunger more than satisfied. Other key value ingredients are efficient and timely service, and, of course, the unusual theme or ambiance that transform the simplest of meals into an experience. To argue which of these is most important is academic. Professionals must address them all. However, those who are most successful provide their guests with something more—*the unexpected extra.*

Incorporating unexpected extras into the standard guest experience enhances the price/value relationship. The unexpected extra is a gift of hospitality and transcends commercialism. The symbol is frequently tangible in the foodservice industry. It can be a special salad, an appetizer, or a complimentary beverage or dessert. The gift can also be intangible. It can be personalized attention from the manager in the form of recognition or special assistance.

In their book, *Service America: Doing Business in a New Economy,* Karl Albrecht and Ron Zemke describe this concept as "value-added services" or those peripheral or secondary services that complement and increase the value of the basic service system (*1*). Value-added services must be managed. Managed means that unexpected extras must be planned for and budgeted, implemented, and controlled. The unexpected extra contributes to bonding the seller to the buyer.

Although planned, value-added services must be varied and seem spontaneous to the guest. They must encompass a variety of guests' expectations and not become normal expectations. For example, if what starts out as an "added" service becomes so incorporated into a facility's standard experience package that it becomes expected, it loses the feeling of spontaneity so important in such services.

The facility must find new services to make its offering better than before and better than its competition's. For example, 30 years ago the standard for services in a motel included cleanliness, comfortable furnishings, and security. These basics, together with quiet, were necessary for a good night's sleep. To enhance the value of their facilities, some motels provided black and white television, air conditioning, telephones, and swimming pools.

As these services became standard, expectations innovators added services such as wake-up calls, cable movies, a morning newspaper at the door, valet service, and transportation to and from the airport. As consumers came to expect such extra services, motels evolved into motor hotels and needed new services to exceed guest expectations. They provided remote control television, terrycloth bathrobes, personal care appliances (hair blowers), luxury toiletries, saunas, health clubs, jogging trails, stocked bars, free breakfasts, and VIP cocktail parties.

What was once viewed as value-added extras in a restaurant, i.e. consistent cleanliness, quality food, and efficient service, are no longer unique selling propositions. All successful facilities provide such fundamentals and would not be in business without them. Having unique tasting food, efficient service, and a clean facility are part of the "expected" dining experience. Value-added extras, such as complimentary food and non-food items, are used to enhance the qualitative aspect of the price/value relationship. Today, the focus is on providing service "extras" to ensure the loyalty of guests, increase guest counts, and be able to increase prices, thereby increasing the restaurant's profitability.

Value-added Services: The Human Dimension

The parameters of value-added services are part of a company's policies and procedures (i.e. there are guidelines to providing them.) But, the most effective value-added services stem from the buyer's "feelings" which arise out of the caring way in which the services are provided. It is in the relationships restaurants build with their guests. Creating good relationships with guests is the human side of giving service that exceeds expectations. Frequently, these are small acts of friendliness and caring which result in immediacy of action. Consider the following examples:

- A service person suggests that a guest order salmon because the salmon was fresh that morning.

- A host notices that a party of two are carrying their briefcases into the dining room. The host recognizes that they plan to conduct business over their meal and seats them at a quiet, out-of-the-way table for four to ensure their comfort.

- A server, seeing that the children in a party are restless, brings crackers, crayons, and a coloring book to the table to occupy them while their order is being prepared.

Acting Before Being Asked

The contact personnel in each of these situations anticipated their guests' needs and took action before being asked. Anticipation and action are two critical service elements in relationship building. Service people make their guests' interests their priority and act accordingly. This is the essence of hospitality. It is the relationship that results from *noticing, caring,* and *behaving.* Unexpected service extras result from empathetic service people who are looking for their guests' special needs ("HOT" spots—hospitality opportunity times) and behave in some extraordinary way to satisfy them. These actions often require no tangible costs.

Types of Value-added Services

The possible value-added services in a restaurant are infinite, and therefore no policy manual can contain the vast array of hospitality opportunities. The following are among the most important service extras that contribute to guest satisfaction.

Attending to Personal Details

The ego must be fed, as well as the appetite. Although all guests receive the same high standards of service from a restaurant, contact employees make the difference by attending to guests' ego needs. Ego needs include recognition, status, affection, and appreciation. For example, remembering and calling guests by name, or remembering guests' food preferences are just two personal service details that communicate to guests that they are important. These, above all, create a bond of loyalty between a guest and the establishment.

Restaurants use different strategies for personalizing the service experience. A table service restaurant may have a policy of obtaining the guests' last names at the host stand and requiring service personnel to address guests by their names during the dining experience. A casual or fast-service facility may use guests' first names (instead of numbers) to let them know their orders are ready.

Value-added policies must be backed up by systems. For example, to ensure that even new customers are addressed by name, the host at one fine restaurant gives name cards to the captains (24). Another establishment prides itself on its servers' response time to guest demands. The facility has a card on each table that informs guests the service staff is a team and any employee in the vicinity of the table can be asked for assistance (16). To serve regular guests more effectively, some facilities keep guest records and note personal requirements.

Restaurants provide value-added services when they attend to the special needs of particular consumer groups such as children, older customers, the disabled, guests celebrating special occasions, business people, those seeking a "mini" vacation by dining out, guests looking for sociability, solitary diners, or out-of-town visitors.

Providing for Children

For families with young children, dining out can be fun or a disastrous experience. The difference depends upon a restaurant's ability to adapt its service to the special needs of this group. Children have strong restaurant loyalties, as anyone who has tried to drive past nationally advertised fast-service establishments with a hungry child can verify. There are 51.8 million children 14 years or younger in this country and they are a powerful market force. Their numbers and ages influence where their families dine.

Restaurants provide value-added service when they use techniques to make family dining experiences more convenient and enjoyable. Strategies frequently used include:

- *A children's menu.* Appealing menus for children consist of plain, popular, easily eaten foods that have been selected with good nutrition in mind. Portions on children's menus are usually smaller and priced differently than adult portions.

- *Booster seats, high chairs, seats that attach to tables (that meet federal safety standards), child-sized utensils and glassware, and disposable bibs.* These items are always appreciated. Some restaurants appealing to young families place changing tables in restrooms.

- *Entertainment.* To make the wait for food more pleasant, many facilities offer entertaining distractions for children up to a certain age (usually 10 or 12 years). Special menus, books or place-mats to color, games to play, and new puzzles to solve are some of the methods used. At one facility, the children's menu is a coloring book that is given to the child along with a box of crayons that can be taken home (27). Large video screens (featuring cartoons) or mechanical rides are popular in some family restaurants. A few restaurants that cater to families have built play areas on their premises.

- *Small gifts.* Restaurants may give children complimentary gifts or tokens for vending machines that contain safe items such as stickers or small toys. Other establishments let children choose similar products from boxes, such as those decorated to look like treasure chests.

- *Fast and friendly service.* Many restaurants have operational procedures which facilitate faster service for children by serving their orders before the adults in their party. In some facilities where this is not possible, restaurateurs have trained servers to be responsive to children by being friendly, bringing beverages quickly, or giving children a small, non-food trinket.

- *Seating that suits the needs of the establishment.* Restaurateurs are divided in opinion on segregated seating for families with children.

Some feel it makes these families more comfortable and enhances the ambiance for other guests; while others feel segregated seating is unnecessary or counterproductive.

- *Something special.* Many restaurants gear promotions (birthdays, holidays, or other) to children to attract their parents to the facility. One company runs cooking classes for children ages 7 to 14 in which the children learn to prepare different menu items. Parents are invited to the last class in the series and their children prepare and serve them a meal (*30*). Other restaurateurs have found that early-dinner specials are appreciated by this group.

Showing Consideration to Older Guests

People in the older market segments eat out an average of twice a week and 25 percent of them would like to eat out even more frequently (*26*). Providing them with extra value results in extra business. The newly created "Grandparent's Day" is "Second only to Mother's Day as a dining-out occasion" (*13*). Older customers appreciate:

- *Specially-priced early lunches and dinners.* Generally, retired and older guests prefer to eat earlier and are attracted to a facility with price specials.

- *Better lighting.* A National Restaurant Association survey of senior citizens who dine out revealed that the most frequent complaint about restaurants is dim lighting (*26*).

- *Buffet-style service.* Many older guests enjoy having a selection of foods and prefer to determine their own serving sizes.

- *Half-size portions.* These are appreciated by guests with small appetites.

- *Food sharing.* The appetite and budgetary requirements of older guests can be better accommodated if they can share an entrée without being embarrassed or order several appetizers rather than an entrée.

- *Special attention to dietary restrictions on sodium, fat, cholesterol, and sugar intake.* Older guests are loyal to establishments that cater to their health needs.

- *Recognition, respect, and patience for "seniors."* Older guests especially appreciate recognition and respect, and a friendly atmosphere.

They prefer seating that is easy to get in and out of, brighter lighting, larger print on menus, more contrast between the print on the menu and the menu's color, extra time to read the menu or the bill, easy access to restrooms and coat racks, and well-lighted parking lots. The rapport "Between the seniors and the employees is also very important. Give them a choice between a server who knows the vegetable of the day or a server who will look at pictures of their grandchildren, they will pick the latter every time" (25).

Ensuring Access for Disabled Guests

Disabled guests, whether they are blind, hearing-impaired, wheelchair-bound, or have some other impairment, are entitled to the same satisfaction as other guests. But, they have unique requirements necessitated by their disabilities. Of course, the facility must be barrier-free and conform to all government regulations regarding access. Some restaurants go further to provide exceptional value-added service to this group. For example they

- Provide braille and large-type menus.

- Have tables that are high enough to accommodate wheelchairs.

- Provide personnel to carry orders to the tables in cafeterias and self-service restaurants.

- Have special training programs geared to creating personnel awareness and sensitivity for those who are disabled.

In an effort to serve the estimated 22 million hearing-impaired people in this country (21), some take-out, home delivery, and other facilities that require telephone contact with guests use a telecommunications device for the deaf (TDD). "A TDD has a typewriter keyboard and accepts a telephone receiver. The user dials the number of a friend or business also equipped with a TDD and when the other party answers, types in a message. After reading the opening statement, the call recipient can key in a response and the process is repeated until the conversation ends" (8).

When restaurant personnel agree to a special request from a disabled guest, they must be sure to deliver exactly what was promised. One disabled guest called a large restaurant with seating on two floors to make a reservation for a large party. The guest explained that a table located on the same floor as the entrance was necessary because he was the host and was unable to climb stairs. Unfortunately, when the group arrived at the facility, they were told their beautifully set table was upstairs. The group angrily left the restaurant and went elsewhere for dinner.

Making Memorable "Special Occasion" Dining

Restaurants are places for celebrating. Guests, whether they are celebrating birthdays, holidays, anniversaries or other occasions, or are seeking to relive and/or create memories or memorable dining experiences, are dependent upon personalized service. Restaurants catering to special occasion dining must be prepared with value-added extras to make events truly memorable.

There are many opportunities to make birthday celebrations enjoyable. In some operations, groups of servers gather to sing "Happy Birthday" when birthday cakes are presented. Others announce the occasion over the public address (PA) system, on a marquee or computerized sign, and so forth. Frequently, they offer the celebrant complimentary or discounted meals, drinks, or desserts. The free birthday meal is usually designated for the celebrant only. One operation determines the discount by the celebrant's age: a twenty-five year old would receive a 25 percent discount, a fifty year old would receive a 50 percent discount and so on (27). A Florida restaurant has a "preferred customer club." Members receive a complimentary bottle of champagne on their birthdays (2).

Many restaurants offer special products that are not on the menu and are only available to birthday celebrants. One operation gives celebrants who are of legal drinking age special cocktails. "The colorful liquor and fruit drink (unavailable on the menu) comes in a 30-ounce brandy snifter that understandably attracts attention from patrons when the server presents it" (2).

Some facilities give birthday celebrants complimentary non-food items such as flowers, balloons, instamatic pictures of themselves on birthday cards, and other small gifts. Other facilities keep a file of customers' birthdates and send out cards shortly before their birthdays. They may also include coupons for discounted or complimentary meals in these cards.

Pictures are also given as mementos to remind guests of their dining out experience and encourage them to return to the restaurant. In addition to giving celebrants Instamatic pictures, one restaurant hangs duplicate photographs on the walls of the facility's waiting area (2).

Adding Festivity to Holiday Celebrations

Holidays in a restaurant can be joyous, carefree occasions for guests when the right value-added services are offered. Many restaurants provide festive decorations, special menus, and entertainment for holiday celebrations. Christmas, historical, geographic, and ethnic themes are especially popular. One restaurant sends patrons letters that may be redeemed for a complimentary bottle of vintage champagne for holiday celebrations (27). Another facility has an employee dressed up as Santa Claus who visits each table and gives out gifts.

Chocolates and other candies for Easter, small flags on the Fourth of July, and noisemakers and hats on New Year's Eve are just a few of the complimentary items that restaurants frequently use to add excitement and value to holiday dining.

Providing for Business People

Business people patronize restaurants for a variety of reasons—to eat a replacement meal while they are away from home, to conduct a business meeting, or to entertain guests in conjunction with a business meeting. Successful operations recognize that the types of special services business people require depend on the reason they are dining out.

Frequently, price is less the object than service. Many business people are on expense accounts when traveling and look for comfortable and convenient restaurants to compensate them for the inconvenience and hardship of business travel. Quick service and convenience for the replacement meal, quieter, more private areas to conduct business, and attentive service to ensure schedules can be met are all important to this group. Anticipating these needs and exceeding expectations is critical for a restaurant to attract and keep the business trade.

Some restaurants meet the needs of business guests by offering private rooms for meetings or other functions. Other establishments provide newspapers, business magazines, and use of telephones. One renowned restaurant installed a private phone at a regular guest's luncheon table (10).

Many restaurants meet business customers' need for replacement meals by offering quick delivery of specified items. "Express lunches" are especially popular. Typically, these involve special entrées or offerings from a limited menu. Service delivery varies for these types of meals. One establishment guarantees delivery in eight minutes or the lunch is free (23). A New Jersey restaurant has a private dining room for business guests. Lunch is served between noon and one o'clock, with a guarantee of 45-minute in-and-out service (*27*).

Restaurants are finding that, in addition to the luncheon trade, business people can be an important part of the breakfast and dinner trades. Business people used to regard breakfast in a restaurant as a convenient replacement meal. However, breakfast business meetings have become popular. Executives are finding that "Breakfast meetings are easier to attend because, unlike lunches, they do not break up the business day" (*28*). One operation offers a business breakfast package. In addition to coffee, tea, juices, breads, pastries, and fresh fruit, guests may choose from a variety of offerings from rich, indulgent foods such as foie gras, caviar, smoked salmon, and pastries stuffed with eggs to fat-, sodium- or calorie-reduced products that include egg substitutes and low-fat yogurt. Extra services provided by the facility include placing thermal carafes of coffee on the table, providing complimentary newspapers, and allowing the free use of a telephone for local calls. Even the menu is an added value—it is also a note pad (*28*).

In addition to serving business people in the facility, some restaurants are providing service by offering off-premises catering. To some operations, "Corporate catering is particularly important because it helps restaurants fill their slower weekday time slots" (*14*).

Facilitating the Escape—Meal Time as a Mini-vacation

Restaurants provide guests with "mini-vacations" by shutting out the outside world. They create a fantasy environment using special decor, food, and employees in costumes to create a theme. Chart 5.1 lists a few of the themes used by restaurants to provide an "escape" experience.

Employees add extra value to the experience when they perform their duties in accordance with the ambiance. When the mood is romantic, lowered voices are appreciated; when there's much festivity, employees enhance the atmosphere by being extroverted and playful.

Although carrying out the theme entertains guests, atmosphere is never a substitute for quality food, service, and value. A frequent criticism of theme restaurants is that the decor is great, the menu is clever, but the food could be better. Also, restaurateurs cannot rely on the creativity of the original concept to guarantee long-term success. They need to creatively adapt the restaurant over time to keep customers interested and meet their needs for new experiences. Some themes, nautical and Early American for example, are traditional favorites and require only occasional cosmetic upgrading. Other themes

---

Chart 5.1. Food and Decor for Popular Restaurant Themes

Cafe. Lighter foods, travel posters, small tables, informal atmosphere, servers in berets, and French music.

Country Inn. American regional food, fireplaces, upholstered chairs, candles on tables, stone floors and walls, and country antiques.

Far East. Chinese, Japanese, Korean, Thai, or other Asian foods, lanterns, oriental artwork and music, windchimes, rice paper wall dividers, chopsticks, and Oriental china and serviceware.

Garden, Greenhouse, or Patio. Natural foods, open spaces, wicker furniture, floral fabrics, glass-top tables, and trees and plants.

Good Old Days. American food favorites, player pianos, popcorn machines, old photographs and artifacts, and old-time music.

Irish Pub. Irish food, large bar area, specialty beers and ales, dart boards, limited menu cards, and Irish music.

Mexican. Mexican food, Spanish-influenced decorations, terra cotta floors, baskets, cacti, servers in serapes and sombreros, and strolling guitarists.

Nautical. Seafood, porthole windows, fishnets and other fishing equipment, lanterns, treasure chests, old maps and ships' logs, and servers dressed in sailor suits.

Polynesian. Polynesian food, wooden floors, fishnets, torches, tiki statues of folklore gods and birds, servers and entertainers dressed in traditional costumes, dancers, island music, floor shows, and flowers for customers.

Rathskeller. Traditional German food, costumes, and music, beer steins, and hanging sausages and wursts.

Trattoria. Italian food, red and white checkered tablecloths, hanging wine bottles, intimate tables with candles and wine bottles, and Italian music.

---

have shorter life cycles and the restaurant may require an entirely new concept. *Good food, friendly service, and value never wear out and add long life to themes.*

Accommodating Solo Diners

In the past, many restaurants have been insensitive to the needs of solo guests, but with the growing number of single persons they are beginning to recognize the value of these patrons. "Restaurants are once again emphasizing counter seating as an accommodation to solo guests—many of whom fear the intimidating prospect of occupying a table alone. Sushi-bar retrofits, oyster-bar extensions of liquor bars, communal table arrangements, counter-fronted exhibition kitchens, and special service considerations at regular dining tables all serve to address the needs of single diners" (*20*).

Special services restaurants are offering solo guests include:

- *Showing solo diners the same level of hospitality shown to groups.* The size of the party is not necessarily an indication of the size of the cover. One manager comments, "I've had single diners order a bottle of Dom Pérignon for themselves, and right there you're talking about a $150 cover" (*20*). Other operators have found that solo business diners often dine alone one night, but return to the restaurant at some other time as part of a group. Regardless of how much they spend, solo guests deserve the same treatment given to other guests.

- *Seating solo diners appropriately.* Solo guests resent automatically being seated at tiny tables located in unfavorable, noisy, often dark locations such as next to the kitchen and restroom entrances. They deserve the same seating considerations as groups, and appreciate comfort and a pleasant view. Solo guests may prefer to read, and therefore require tables with higher light intensity.

- *Providing social interaction.* Some establishments seat solo diners near each other, so they may converse if they so desire. Other facilities have communal tables for solo diners who prefer not to dine alone. One restaurant refers to its communal table as *tavola degli amici* (table of friends). Another restaurant has a service policy that requires the manager to greet solo diners at some point during their meal to ensure that they are comfortable.

- *Anticipating the speed of service desired.* Some solo diners want only a quick replacement meal; others want to relax after a hard day or linger because they have free time. Servers can look for cues from the guest regarding the pace of the meal, or can ask them in a courteous, friendly manner how quickly they wish to be served.

- *Offering wines by the glass or half-bottle.* Solo diners appreciate when wine and champagne are offered to them in suitable portions by the half-bottle or glass.

- *Providing reading material.* Some restaurants offer newspapers and magazines to solo guests so they are entertained while they await their meals.

Welcoming Tourists

Data from the United States Travel and Tourism Administration (USTTA) indicate that both more Americans and more foreigners are traveling in the United States. The largest number of foreign tourists come from Canada, Mexico, Japan, Great Britain, and West Germany (*18*). Research shows "Vacationers from all major countries except France now list food among their reasons for traveling in the United States" (*19*).

The United States Travel and Tourism Association, along with restaurants throughout the country, have developed programs to promote food to travelers. In 1986, the "America, Catch the Spirit" promotion focused on the diversity of American foods. "From New York City's 'vast spectrum of international cuisines' at 25,000 restaurants to the Pennsylvania Dutch country's 'bountiful servings of souse, schnitzel, and schoofly pie' and from Milwaukee's beer and Polish sausage to Savannah's elegant Old Pink House, 'America, Catch the Spirit' is telling foreign travelers that good U.S. restaurants come in all colors, shapes, and kinds—and in all 50 states" (*19*).

Restaurants contribute to a visitor's vacation experience by providing a touch of regional tastes and serving them in a hospitable manner. Facilities make these visitors feel especially welcome when they have staff available who speak their language, or have menus in other languages to accommodate visitors who have a limited knowledge of English. Tourists also appreciate receiving information about the area in which the restaurant is located. In addition to the complimentary products discussed earlier, some restaurants give tourists souvenirs, such as menu mailers, postcards containing pictures of the restaurant, or a map of the surrounding area.

When employees attend to the personal service details of each step of the service procedure, from the time guests call the restaurant for a reservation to the time they leave the facility, guests receive value-added service.

Compliments of the Restaurant—the Programmed Surprise

Providing complimentary or special products is a popular value-added service policy. Offering complimentary products "Is a practice that generates goodwill, leaving the diner with an impression of [being singled out, important, and pampered. It results in] making paying the check more pleasant—and in the long run helping to generate" (6) repeat business and that all-important word-of-mouth advertising.

Restaurants offer a variety of complimentary products at various times during a guest's dining experience. One restaurant's service policy is to offer hot cider (a specialty of the facility) while guests wait in line on cold nights outside the restaurant. Another provides unique hors d'oeuvres to guests while they are waiting to be seated. These value-added services are an expression of caring. However, they are consumed before the guest leaves the facility and are not carried home. Therefore, in order to be effective gifts, they should be accompanied by experiences and stories that guests can carry away with them.

Programmed Extras that Convey Hospitality

Many establishments offer a variety of breads, rolls, and butters as programmed extras. Others present unusual cheeses, vegetables, and dips as soon as guests are seated. Signature breads and rolls are labor intensive and require much attention if they are going to be memorable. However, preparing a few difficult extras makes it hard for competitors to copy them. One celebrated New York restaurant offers mini-croissants (24), and the Parker House in Boston became world famous for the rolls bearing its name (7). Restaurateurs offer bread baskets "Filled with sourdough and pumpernickel raisin rolls, sliced Irish soda bread, onion rye bread, Italian bread sticks, and flat bread in plain, poppy, and onion flavors" (7).

Corn, garlic, sourdough, multi-grain, date nut, whole wheat, and cheese breads are popular choices at other facilities. In addition, restaurateurs are emphasizing the freshness of their bread products to make a promise of other good things to come.

Some establishments provide butters flavored with honey, fruit, herbs (parsley, dill, chives, basil, and others) or spices. They are serving sweet butters with honey, cinnamon, lemon, or strawberries with plain breads and rolls, and using stronger herbed butters for coarser-textured breads.

Complimentary snacks and hors d'oeuvres are also prevalent and range from simple to elaborate. Snack foods such as freshly prepared nuts, popcorn, pretzels, cheese crackers, potato chips with dip, and tortilla chips with salsa are popular. Some facilities offer impressive complimentary crudité (fresh vegetable) platters, consisting of such items as cherry tomatoes, and sliced cauliflower, carrots, broccoli, peppers, celery, cucumbers, and zucchini. Dips accompanying these platters are often made with sour or cream cheese. Fresh, unblemished, quality vegetables sliced in attractive shapes such as spears, sticks, flowers, and wheels add to the appeal of crudité platters.

Complimentary beverages may be given at any time during the meal. Some restaurants offer complimentary refills for soft drinks and coffee. They may place a decanter of coffee on the table, set up a self-service refill area, or make servers responsible for refills.

Perhaps the most celebrated gift of hospitality was offered by a famous club in New York. The restaurant managers set aside fine bottles of wine in their cellar to celebrate the births of members' children. The bottles were opened when the members celebrated their children's twenty-first birthdays at the club.

Some operators are experimenting with other types of complimentary items. They may give guests unusual foods or beverages that are not on the menu, especially favorite food items uniquely prepared (french-fried asparagus or zucchini bread for example). Sometimes, they offer complimentary liquor (where permitted by law) with ethnic appetizers. A one-ounce portion is sufficient. Some examples of this include:

- Russian vodka with Moscow salad.

- Saké or plum wine with rumaki or tempura.

- Ouzo with spanakopita or hummus spread.

- Tequilla with nachos.

A complimentary réléve served between courses is also used to surprise guests. For this treat, many chefs choose lemon sorbet served on accordion-cut lemon halves or other seasonal fruit sorbets because they are light, refreshing, and prepare the palate for the next course.

Providing a Lasting Impression—Dessert

Some experts feel guests are more likely to remember complimentary foods when they are presented at the end of the meal. Dessert items have become one of the most popular forms of complimentary products. Restaurant offerings range from unusual mints (even jelly beans) presented with the guest check or at the cash register to plates of fresh fruits served with cookies and candies at tables. "There is no rule to quantity, either. [The only rule is that the gift be unique and thus remembered.] In some restaurants the plate or stand on the table is richly laden with cookies and petit fours, chocolates, and candied fruit. Elsewhere one fine chocolate per guest is offered when the check is presented" (6).

Complimentary dessert treats include:

- *Mints.* Refreshing jelly-filled, peppermint, or soft chewy mints have become familiar offerings in many restaurants. Small packets of mints provided with orders have been used as an added surprise by take-out or drive-through facilities.

- *Chocolate-dipped fruit.* Fresh whole strawberries, banana slices, or dried apricots dipped in fine chocolate are popular choices.

- *Miniature danish or other pastries.* Fruit or cheese danish, small éclairs, and petit fours have guest appeal.

- *Chocolates.* "Chocolate truffles have become an especially appealing postprandial nibble—one that reinforces an impression of quality and luxury" (*6*). Other types of chocolates are popular as well. One restaurant serves an unusual product—coffee with chocolate sticks "Made from chocolate semipuff pastry dough that is rolled in cinnamon and sugar and dipped in white and dark chocolate" (*4*).

- *Cookies.* Almond, fortune, macaroon, palmier, and chocolate chip are just a few types of popular cookies offered.

- *Ice cream bon bons.* Bon bons filled with chocolate, vanilla, or other flavors of ice cream are favorites of both adults and children.

- *Fresh fruits.* These are served whole or sliced and are often accompanied by cookies. One fine restaurant presents a basket of seasonal fruit to each table at the end of the meal (*9*). Another restaurateur has a barrel of fruit near the exit so guests can take a piece as they leave.

- *Candied fruit.* Some operations provide candied fruit or fruit peel because they are unique, sweet, and satisfying items.

Making Use of Non-Food Items

Complimentary items are not always food or beverage products; they may be non-food items that are a part of a promotional campaign, such as matchbooks, balloons, and cocktail stirrers that bear the establishment's name or logo. Other facilities give away miniature menus, monographed ash trays, or glassware in which specialty drinks have been served.

Facilities are careful to select those complimentary items that reflect their image. A single rose may be appropriate for an upscale restaurant, but a "funky" T-shirt may be best for a theme establishment.

Some facilities send newsletters to people on their mailing lists. Newsletters are used to congratulate guests on various achievements or special occasions; spotlight what's new in the restaurant; discuss food; or give advice about food preparation or dining out. Other facilities mark occasions by sending regular guests notes of congratulations or flowers (*10*).

Although complimentary products add value to the dining experience, they can lose their value if not presented as a sincere gift of hospitality. They can also backfire if not discreetly presented, making other guests feel left out. Gifts, when not presented for a justifiable reason to all guests, must be provided tactfully and with little notice outside of that particular party. Otherwise, others will feel slighted. When the unexpected extra is programmed for all, guests should receive the same complimentary products in the same amounts, regardless of whether they are regulars or new patrons.

When guests are served complimentary items, they should be informed (by servers, signs, or other printed materials) that the treat is a gift of the manager or an individual that represents the restaurant. If the give-away is for a limited period, this should also be stated. For example, in offering a complimentary item a server might say, "Would you like to try a stuffed clam? It's on-the-house this evening." If qualifying statements are not made, guests will expect the same treat on a subsequent dining occasion and be disappointed when it is not provided. This leads to guest dissatisfaction and detracts from the value-added service.

Intangible Gifts of Hospitality

Restaurateurs provide a gift of hospitality and exceed the guests' expectations when services go beyond what guests normally expect from restaurants. For example, guests entering fast-service establishments want convenient, quick, quality meals. However, one fast-service chain company surprised its guests by changing its image for an evening. "Tablecloths were spread, managers wore tuxedos, and a violinist strolled. Traffic increased 35 percent" (*7*).

Lodging establishments are also recognizing traditional room service is not enough for some guests who want guarantees that their food will be served at a particular time. For example, several companies offer guests the option of ordering breakfast the night before by filling out order cards or telephoning in orders. Another company has decided to take a different approach to provide quick, convenient meals. "An 'inflight kitchen' operates every morning in an elevator equipped with a radio operator, toasters, warming trays, and coffee and tea service" (*15*).

To indulge guests who want to linger over dessert, many restaurateurs have designed special dessert sections in their facilities so that guests can enjoy desserts and after-dinner drinks in a relaxing, comfortable environment without feeling pressured that their tables are needed for other guests. Guests dining at one fine restaurant are escorted to the dessert table and then upstairs to a separate room where they can leisurely enjoy dessert, coffee, tea, or after-dinner drinks. According to the owner, "It's like retiring to the library for cognac" (*4*).

A Florida restaurateur opened a dessert restaurant upstairs from the regular dining room. The dessert restaurant has private booths which are "Equipped with color television and stereophonic speakers. Guests can elect to watch network or closed-circuit channels or listen to any of 11 channels of music, ranging from classical to country. In addition, they can tune in to the live entertainment by the baby grand piano" (*17*).

Other facilities indulge their guests by giving customized treatment. One operator has a computer listing of guests' favorite dishes and special requests and calls them when the restaurant plans to serve these foods. According to the operator, "People like to be called at their home of office when their favorites are going to be served. It's many phone calls, but well worth the effort because of the increased business it brings us" (*3*).

Other restaurateurs are proud of their ability to offer guests individualized services. One fine New York restaurant always leaves a few tables open when booking reservations, so it can accommodate regulars at a moment's notice. In addition, the restaurant's car is used to take patrons home or to the theater and to send care packages to patrons who are ill (*24*). Variations on this theme include having a limousine pick-up and delivery service for special occasions; or providing free, luxurious private dining rooms for celebrations or meetings.

At another restaurant, a guest remarked to the manager that a glaze for a party cake she had made did not turn out right. The manager spoke to the chef, and a glaze was delivered to the guest's home in time for the party that night (*5*).

Restaurants can make guests feel special by featuring the local business person of the month in the lobby or using guests' recipes and recognizing them on the menu. Other methods include decorating the walls with pictures of guests and naming menu items after them, local businesses, or school teams.

"Giving-away" Recipes and Wine Information

Restaurants also provide value-added service by sharing recipe or food-service information with guests. Explaining how a dish is prepared or what ingredients create the flavor in a dish makes them feel special. These are valuable techniques for encouraging guests to return to the restaurant. Some restaurants provide guests with recipes for menu items. One restaurant holds free cooking classes that are followed by specially-priced meals. A New York restaurant gives guests who order wine a card bearing a reproduction of the wine label and information about the vintage (27).

Making it Their Way—Special Food Preparation

Restaurants must deal with requests that may or may not be health-related. One restaurant owner had the chef prepare a bluefish that a guest had caught and brought into the restaurant (9). Another restaurant prides itself on being "The largest à la carte restaurant in the world" (24). According to the owners, they do their utmost to provide guests with whatever foods they want whenever they want them (24).

Preparing food according to customer requests is an important value-added service. From fast-service chain companies that tell guests to enjoy food prepared "their way," to the finest tablecloth operations, restaurants that will prepare anything a guest desires, given a reasonable amount of time, are recognizing the importance of attending to special orders.

The Healthy Way

A survey by The American Heart Association revealed that more restaurants are trying to accommodate requests for health-related special food preparations. These requests include (22, 29):

- *Eliminating an ingredient or product.* Some guests prefer that their food be prepared without MSG (monosodium glutamate), salt or other seasonings, gravy, butter, or sour cream. Others request that some of these products be served on the side.

- *Changing the portion size.* More guests want smaller portions or want to share menu selections with others in their party. Restaurants are responding by offering items on the menu that are meant to be shared or are making foods available in different portion sizes.

- *Substituting one product for another.* Guests often request margarine instead of butter; low-fat or skim milk instead of whole milk; salad or vegetables in place of a side dish that is higher in calories; lemon juice or vinegar instead of salad dressing; and fruit instead of a richer dessert.

- *Using a different preparation method.* Some guests require that foods be cooked in vegetable oil instead of butter; or be broiled, baked, steamed, or poached rather than be fried or sautéed.

Labeling Menus or Products

As a value-added service, an increasing number of restaurants are presenting guests with ingredient, calorie, or other nutritional information. Some restaurants are adding "light" foods to their menus and are providing calorie counts for these foods as well. Many companies are receiving more requests from business and other guests for lower calorie meals. One hotel foodservice manager comments, "We had hundreds and hundreds or requests from men and women traveling 50 or 60 times a year who were tired of gaining weight" (5).

Major fast-service chains are making brochures available to guests that contain nutrition information about their products. Some also offer information about the cooking methods they use.

The value-added services described in this chapter are just a few of the services offered. Restaurants that creatively provide these and other types of services based on their guests' needs will be more likely to achieve and maintain success.

6

Effective Communication Facilitates Service

The Basics

One guest complains the service is too slow, another is calling for the server because the wrong entrée was delivered. A third thinks the wine is off and is demanding to see the manager—a typical bad day in the restaurant business is underway. Yet, each of these service problems can be solved, or at least prevented from going from bad to worse, if an effective communication program is in effect.

Effective communication is a term heard increasingly as the restaurant industry becomes more professional, specialized, and technological. But, exactly what is effective communication? It has been defined as "The process by which meanings are perceived and understandings reached. It is the process by which management induces [satisfying] action" (2). At its most basic level, communication is the passing of an idea from one person to another. People communicate whenever they interact with others.

Effective communication occurs when a person receiving a communication gets the message intended by the sender. How the message is constructed affects the communication process. A message may travel through many types of communication channels, including sight, hearing, touch, smell, or taste. Verbal messages should be clear, concise, and in the language of the receiver.

Whether communication is formal (governed by organizational policies and procedures) or informal (casual conversations or body language) in a restaurant, it must contain a caring message. Communication must be managed because it affects the very survival of the business. The basis of effective communication is hiring people who are gifted in language—both spoken and acted. Formal communication in an organization depends on a strong company philosophy and goal statement, reinforced by written policies and procedures that are made known to employees. Frequently, employees are presented with this information in company training sessions and in company training manuals, handbooks, or other printed or audiovisual materials. Informal employee communication occurs in casual conversations among employees and guests, through messages conveyed by body language, or along the company grapevine.

To provide exceptional service, an optimum amount of accurate information must flow through an organization. Those who manage the guest experience spend 75 to 85 percent of their time on the job communicating (6). Delivery systems require a myriad of accurate instructions and follow-through. In every way, effective communication improves the dining experience and contributes to the difference between poor and exceptional service.

Various types of communication are necessary in a facility, including one-to-one conversations, group meetings, and using printed, visual, and audio materials. But, restaurant managers, employees, and guests have diverse backgrounds and psychological makeups, and very different roles in the facility. Since it is the restaurant personnel who are providing guest service, they bear the responsibility (in accordance with their roles in the organization) for making sure messages are understood. Managers have to communicate with their employees and guests in an appropriate tone; employees have to consider what they are actually communicating to guests, so guests always feel "in the right."

Communicators should make only those promises they can keep. When managers hint to employees about promotions, extra time off, or any other job advantage, it raises their expectations. Managers also need to keep their promises to guests. If expectations are not met, employees and guests become more dissatisfied, creating a new set of problems.

Meetings are especially effective for explaining new situations or restaurant policies; giving information; presenting and solving problems; or simply building morale ("We need to work as a team to make next year better"). Meetings are also useful for recognizing outstanding job performance ("Thanks for making this the best year ever").

Preparation is the key element in the effective handling of a group meeting of any size. It entails a clear, concise statement of the subject matter, an effective method of presenting the information, and an evaluation of the audience.

Written materials offer several advantages over spoken words. They are permanent records that can be stored for reference. This permanence makes written materials more credible, useful as a legal tool, and seemingly more objective and authoritative. Additionally, people often take written information more seriously and attend to it more carefully.

Written materials also are efficient. They offer a quick, inexpensive means of reaching large groups. They are convenient information sources which can be used before, during, or after meetings.

Audiocassettes, videotapes, slides, films, and transparencies are finding increased favor among all types of business organizations. Many restaurants use audio or audiovisual materials as training tools or for business presentations; audiocassettes and various visual media are also popular for providing guest entertainment.

It is important to ensure that these communication tools be effective when they are used. Audiences should be able to see or hear (as appropriate); materials should be accurate, up-to-date, and interesting; equipment should be available and in working condition. Trainees form negative images of their new employer when they are shown old training tapes. Guests at a restaurant do not appreciate listening to the same section of a song repeatedly or facing a "snowy" television screen.

Improving Restaurant Communication

Business is booming, service is efficient, employees have team spirit, and guests leave the restaurant smiling. These are indications that effective communication is occurring at a facility. But, how can a manager know for certain? General indications are not enough. Managers need to systematically assess the impact of communication in their facilities to ensure that continuous quality service is provided.

But, the many benefits of effective communication, like those of quality service, are intangible, and therefore, hard to evaluate. What causes people to respond to messages as they do? Why might one newspaper restaurant review generate increased traffic, while a complex, expensive advertising campaign fail to produce a single new guest?

Despite the many theories offered as to why people respond positively or negatively to communication, no one can guarantee that a certain type of communication will yield the expected result. The factors involved are too numerous.

To evaluate the communication quality within the restaurant, managers must have a system for observing what is being communicated and obtaining feedback from both employees and guests. One-to-one conversations provide the quickest feedback. As an issue becomes more complicated or as the organization or group becomes larger, feedback is more difficult to get and measure. In this case, a more formal means of acquiring feedback, such as employee and guest surveys or suggestion forms, may be required.

Another way to measure the effectiveness of communication is to evaluate informal messages. Is too much inaccurate information and rumor being passed along the grapevine? This is often an indication that not enough essential information is being provided to employees by formal communication sources. It can also indicate that information is not being passed on at the proper time or in the correct manner.

Some managers believe the grapevine can be used to their advantage, since it has been proven that it spreads news rapidly and is accurate 90 to 95 percent of the time (6). One manager ascertains which servers cannot keep a confidence and regularly passes on facts to these servers in anticipation that the information quickly will reach other staff members.

When Problems Occur

Effective communication is always necessary to provide guest service, but becomes critical when a restaurant experiences employee or guest problems. Bad word-of-mouth can destroy a business. A guest who has had an unsatisfactory experience in a restaurant is likely to tell 10 people about it (4).

Dealing with a problem begins by evaluating it. This is accomplished by:

- Verifying a problem actually exists.

- Defining the problem.

- Obtaining as much information about the situation as possible.

- Categorizing the problem as one facility personnel can handle or one that requires outside professional help (legal, medical).

- Choosing the best method of handling the problem (person-to-person, letter, telephone, or group meeting).

- Creating a positive atmosphere by being calm, courteous, helpful, and efficient.

- Dealing in specifics and remaining objective.

- Avoiding inappropriate reactions, such as hostility.

Once a manager or employee establishes that a problem does in fact exist, the possible solutions need to be considered immediately. Attempting to solve even a simple problem cannot be put off, because ignoring situations generally makes them harder to deal with later on.

Effective communication is always a part of problem-solving. In providing restaurant service, personnel deal with problems associated with guest relations, employee relations, and emergencies.

When a Guest Complains

Customer complaints are a fact of life in the restaurant industry. A steak is over-cooked, food is spilled on a guest's clothing, or a reservation is not recorded, are among the many, sometimes unavoidable, events that cause guests to complain.

Restaurant personnel typically handle guest complaints on a one-to-one basis. Responses to these complaints must always be sincere, courteous, and immediate. In addition to listening to complaints and making an apology, many employees offer complimentary items to help soothe hurt feelings. Often, a free drink or dessert, a rose from a bouquet, or a meal on the house are more effective and more appreciated than verbal appeasement. When complaints are handled well, guests can leave a restaurant even more satisfied with the facility than before the problem occurred. Chart 6.1 shows one model for providing effective service when dealing with guest complaints.

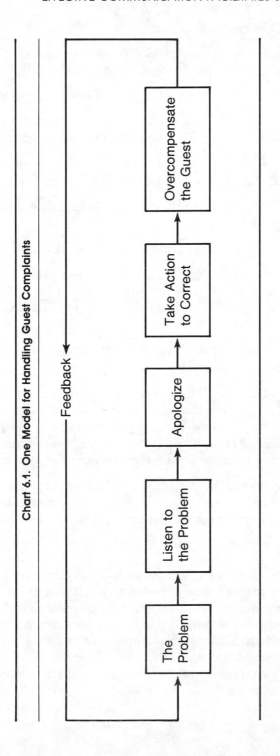

Chart 6.1. One Model for Handling Guest Complaints

Telephone Complaints

Diplomacy and communication skills are also needed when employees handle complaints by telephone. Employees should:

- Answer the telephone quickly and not keep the customer waiting for assistance.

- Write down the caller's name, telephone number, and address as soon as possible.

- Attend to and note what the caller has to say.

- Using a low key, soothing voice, respond in a courteous, non-judgemental manner.

- Be tactful and avoid sounding irritated by the call.

- Use apologetic phrases to show concern ("We're sorry you had a problem. We'll do everything we can to make sure it never happens again," or "Thanks for letting us know. Calls such as yours are really helpful").

- Make certain the problem is fully understood before a response or solution is offered.

- Respond or offer the solution. If employees cannot solve specific problems because they are complex or deal with medical or legal issues, they should inform callers that they will get back to them. Employees should immediately pass the information about such calls to those in the facility who can handle them.

- Follow-up on the telephone call as appropriate and according to company policies and procedures. Most facilities send letters; many also offer complimentary items such as drinks or desserts.

Letters to Guests

Studies have shown that the first five lines of any letter get the most attention. The beginning of an effective letter written in response to a guest's complaint conveys that the management is fully aware of and is concerned about the guest's problem. This must be conveyed to the guest, even when managers or employees disagree with the guest's version of an incident. A polite, conciliatory tone often works best, along with a restatement of the problem and an explanation of what can be done to solve it.

Response letters to guests should be personalized, even when they are form letters. Many experts believe appropriately using a guest's name in the text of the letter is beneficial. However, even when their names have been inserted, guests today can spot poorly written computerized form letters. These are rarely an effective communication tool.

Letters can be brief (one page or less) and should be written in a conversational tone. Basic language without difficult words or negative terms is best.

A customer (Jane Smith) writes a complaint letter to a successful restaurant informing the owner that on the previous evening she and her business associates, despite a reservation, were kept waiting for their table for more than an hour. An inadequate response to this letter might read:

December 22, 1987

Smith
123 Main Street
Hillman, Illinois

Dear Customer:

We are responding to your letter of December 17. It is most unfortunate that you were kept waiting for a table, but as you know, this is a very busy time of year for us. You must realize that unexpected problems do occur.

We hope you do not have a similar problem if you return to visit us in the future.

Cordially,

The previous response is not personalized and is too formal. Even though it may be better than no response at all, it does not communicate effectively. A better response might read:

December 22, 1987

Ms. Jane Smith
123 Main Street
Hillman, Illinois

Dear Ms. Smith:

Sorry, sorry, sorry!!! We deeply regret that you and your associates had to wait for a table last Wednesday evening. We sincerely apologize for the inconvenience to you.

Our policy is to honor our reservations. However, the night of your visit the guests occupying the table we set aside for your party lingered far longer than we expected, and we couldn't accommodate you anywhere else in the facility.

We exist to satisfy our guests, and we failed. Ms. Smith, we hope you'll visit us again. Enclosed is a gift certificate to encourage you to do so. We want another opportunity to show you that we can serve you well.

Have a joyous New Year.

Cordially,

Employee-related Communication

Employees are at the center of a restaurant's communication system. They interface with other employees (both above and below them in the organization's hierarchy), guests, or suppliers. Their formal roles in the company and their informal contacts with others determine when their communication is related to areas that affect guest service in the facility.

Employee Behavior

Employee behavior is a primary component of a guest's satisfaction or dissatisfaction with a restaurant. Effective guest communication is facilitated when employees understand their job responsibilities and cooperate with other employees to deliver service as a team. Front-of-house personnel need to relay guests' desires to other personnel, and guest service depends on their ability and willingness to do so effectively.

Good communication among employees is always critical to service, but especially so when role conflicts arise. Two servers may argue as to who is responsible for a particular table, while guests sit waiting for service; kitchen staff and servers may blame each other for incorrect orders, preventing guests from getting their food; or a server may resent being asked by a guest to perform another server's task.

When these role conflicts are persistent, it is a sign that job responsibilities and company policies and procedures have not been communicated effectively to employees and that retraining is necessary.

Employee Turnover

Of course, adequate service depends on having a competent, loyal, and well-trained staff. In many types of facilities, guests enjoy getting to know and being served by familiar personnel. When employee turnover is high, it is another indication that there are communication problems within the organization. When this is a problem for a facility, managers need to evaluate the effectiveness of the communication involved in:

- *Recruiting.* Newspaper advertisements, help-wanted signs, word-of-mouth, educational institutions, and employment agencies send out different types of messages to potential employees and yield different types of job applicants. A restaurant needs to assess which communication channels bring in the best employees.

- *Interviewing techniques.* Personnel executives set the tone for an establishment by what they say to potential employees. Managers need to communicate with those who do the hiring to ensure that the proper messages about the organization are being delivered.

- *Training programs.* Effective training communication helps employees learn to perform their jobs well. Communication techniques need to be evaluated to correct deficiencies.

- *Manager to employee communications.* When managers do a poor job of communicating with employees, employee frustration and dissatisfaction result. Managers need to examine their conversations with employees to evaluate the adequacy of their messages.

Dealing With Accidents and Other Emergencies

Effective communication is critical for preventing accidents and for efficiently handling accidents and other emergencies when they do occur. Common restaurant problems calling for effective communication are: first-aid and medical emergencies; property damage; and theft.

Emergency Service

Emergency situations by their very nature call for fast, capable handling. Handling is facilitated when employees know their roles. Preparation minimizes the chances that employees will make mistakes when they are rushed and upset. Procedures sheets covering the handling of more common emergencies are provided in company handbooks. These procedures are typically explained in company training programs and are reinforced in periodic review sessions. Chart 6.2 contains a sample procedures sheet for use when there is an accident or other crisis.

There are several first-aid emergencies that tend to occur more frequently than others within the restaurant industry. These include: choking on food; falls; unconsciousness; food poisoning; cuts; and burns.

Many facilities keep several recommended first-aid guides on hand for use in emergencies. These are usually stored with first-aid supplies in a convenient location. Every employee should know where to find these materials and supplies and be trained in how to use them. Posters covering the more common first-aid emergencies are frequently posted in prominent locations to afford a quick, easily found reference.

The best posters are ones that are large and colorful with a minimum of print. An approved first-aid poster does a very effective job of illustrating and describing precise first-aid techniques that can be used by non-professionals for handling emergencies. Only one person (preferably in a managerial position) should be responsible for displaying and changing various safety posters and keeping safety program records. Care should be taken that when posters are visible to guests they are not offensive, since they might detract from guests' dining experience.

An essential aspect of emergency first-aid is knowing when a situation can be handled by a lay person and when it is best to leave the victim untouched and call for professional assistance. A good first-aid manual provides details needed to make this decision. Restaurants also need to communicate "safeguarding" procedures to employees. These are the steps that can be taken to minimize the chance of accidents. Steps include:

- Keeping all equipment and furniture exactly where they belong.
- Storing knives and other dangerous items in a safe place.
- Ensuring that flammable items are away from stoves and areas near flames.
- Placing all poisonous materials in containers clearly marked "poison" and storing them separately from food supplies.
- Always maintaining the required temperatures for perishable foods.

Chart 6.2. Handling Accidents and Crises

- Call for emergency assistance immediately: police, an ambulance, a first-aid attendant, or a doctor.

- Learn to identify typical symptoms of sudden-onset illness such as a heart attack, diabetic complications, an epileptic seizure, or a stroke. In a classic example, one woman who suffered a minor stroke was thought to be drunk because her eyes were unfocused and her speech was slurred. Fortunately, an alert manager recognized the true nature of her problem and called for an ambulance. She was lucky and was saved from permanent and tragic damage from what, at first, looked like a minor fall.

- Do not move a customer who has fallen; do not help someone stand up, particularly if the person seems dizzy, confused, or in great pain.

- Provide only emergency first-aid, following established medical procedures in case of a serious or life-threatening situation.

- Do not administer drugs or treatments of any kind, not even simple "home remedies" such as aspirin, cold compresses, or a bandage for a sprain.

- Do not make statements about company insurance coverage or damage recovery policies.

- Do not admit guilt or comment on the dangers of a particular situation by saying such things as, "These steps always get slippery when it's raining outside" or "I knew someone would get hurt here someday."

- Remember that a crowd sometimes gathers in an accident situation, and there may be many witnesses who misunderstand or misinterpret what is said during an emergency.

- Sad as it is to mention, there are some people who "fall" for a living; that is, they create accidents in the hopes of making a large insurance settlement. Clearly, companies do not want to be responsible for such injuries. On the other hand, even "innocent" statements can jeopardize the rights of a person who is hurt in a genuine accident. The best policy to protect the company from insurance scams, and honest customers from losing benefits they might deserve, is to say nothing during an emergency that can be used as evidence pro or con in a trial.

- Educate and train (performance/behavior) all employees to know how to report an emergency or injury immediately and accurately; caution employees about making statements to the injured person, the crowd, the media, or even friends or neighbors. For example, in the case of the stroke victim, suppose one of the servers had told people that the woman was intoxicated—certainly this could be an embarrassing, if not litigious,

---

Chart 6.2. Handling Accidents and Crises (continued)

---

situation for management. Again, the purpose for keeping quiet during and after an emergency is to protect the rights of innocent accident victims and to avoid costly and malicious lawsuits from dishonest people.

- Replacing bulbs as soon as they burn out.

- Repairing frayed electrical cords or any other damaged equipment.

- Checking first-aid supplies to make certain all essentials are always on hand.

- Posting a list of emergency telephone numbers and keeping it up-to-date. Chart 6.3 lists recommended data for such lists.

Property Damage and Loss

Some property damage and loss is bound to occur in any restaurant. Guest property can be lost or damaged when it is checked, or unchecked property can be damaged by guests or employees. Damage to checked property can be avoided by securing the coat check area. Having a responsible employee who makes sure all personal articles are returned to the rightful owner is an asset to any restaurant. Laws concerning liability for checked belongings vary. Posting signs that explain liability for checked belongings in the coat check area is one method many restaurants use to avoid confusion and misunderstandings when losses or damages occur. When checked articles are lost or damaged, the checker should be well versed in company policies and procedures as to how to communicate with guests about the problem.

Accidents do occur in restaurants which result in damage to unchecked guest property. Other guests or employees may be at fault. In such situations, it is critical that employees respond appropriately, tactfully, and apologetically. Apologizing to the guest and offering some type of complimentary item, such as a free meal, drink, or dessert helps calm them and shows the facility's concern. Most restaurateurs also pay for dry cleaning or replacement of the damaged or lost articles and follow up unfortunate mishaps with letters of apology.

Restaurants vary in how they handle guest property damage caused by other guests. Although restaurants usually are not liable when this type of damage occurs, many offer assistance or take other steps to ensure that guests remain calm and tempers don't flare. It is

Chart 6.3. Emergency Telephone Numbers

Hospital

Ambulance service

First-aid squad / paramedics

Poison control center

Manager's home telephone

Owner's home telephone

Local police

State police

Fire department

Doctor

Dentist

Department of Health

Exterminator

Electric company

Gas company

Water company

Lawyer

Insurance agent

Auto towing and emergency repair

Local taxi

Equipment repair:

    Plumber

    Electrician

    Cooking equipment

    Refrigerator and freezer

    Warewashing equipment

    Air conditioning

    Heating

    Other

critical that restaurant personnel remain neutral in disputes among guests. If one patron is arguing with another about damaged property, a manager or other person may want to escort both parties to a more secluded section of the restaurant so other guests are not disturbed.

Theft

Despite security precautions, it is inevitable that some theft will occur in public establishments, such as restaurants. Purses hanging on the backs of chairs or packages placed under tables are tempting targets to thieves. Although restaurants are rarely liable for losses, operators must demonstrate their concern to involved parties when theft does occur. When wallets or purses are stolen, many restaurants offer guests assistance by providing them with a method of getting home and arranging for them to pay their check at a later date.

Sometimes guests accuse employees of theft. A guest may insist that change was given incorrectly, or that personal belongings were stolen by an employee. These situations are especially difficult and should only be handled by owners, managers, or other designated personnel in accordance with company policies and procedures. Disputes concerning change are avoided when restaurants use adequate cash control procedures. When disputes do occur, many operators take the position that "the guest is always right" and offer to adjust the change accordingly.

Robbery

Robbery is defined as, "The taking of property through the use of force or by the threat of force. This may be the physical displaying of a weapon or suspected weapon, the threatened use of a weapon which is concealed or where physical threats to the employees or customers are made" (7). When robberies occur that involve employees and guests, the facility's priority is to protect guests and employees from harm. Experts agree that once a robbery has started, there is no way to stop it. To avoid violence and possible tragedy, employees must communicate a willingness to cooperate with the robbers.

To prevent the likelihood of violence, experts recommend that employees be told the following (5,7):

- *You will be frightened—get hold of your emotions and act calm.* Do what you are told. "Try to remember distinguishing features of the robber; clothing, scars, marks, weapon type, height, weight, hair color, and length. Remember what the robber says" (7).

- *Give the robbers what they request.* Robbers are less likely to injure persons that are willing to cooperate. Don't argue with robbers.

- *Keep the transaction as short as possible.* "The average robbery takes less than 2 minutes. The longer the robbery takes, the more nervous the robber becomes. Handle the procedure as if you were making a sale to a guest" (7).

- *Tell the robber about any sudden moves or surprises.* Inform robbers when it is necessary to make any moves. Also tell them if there are people in the back of the restaurant, or if someone is expected to return to the restaurant. Tell them if a fryer alarm or other surprising noise is about to sound.

- *Don't be a hero and don't try to recover money or articles.* Trying to be heroic endangers innocent people in the facility. Pursuing robbers is also dangerous. Robbers often shoot at pursuers, and police could mistakenly injure them.

- *Don't use, keep, or carry weapons.* Most companies have policies which forbid having weapons in the restaurant.

Immediately after a robbery occurs, it is important to call the police and then notify the manager or owner of the facility. Typically, police request that all persons involved remain in the facility until witness reports are filled out. While waiting for the police, personnel should attempt to calm guests and restore the facility's ambiance as much as possible.

Other Incidents

Restaurants today face the possibility of other types of incidents, including bomb scares and acts of terrorism. This is particularly true for companies developing in the international marketplace. They may be subject to various hostile acts by terrorists who view them as symbols of this country.

Although management is vulnerable to the external environment, they need to create internal options and have plans of action prepared for possible events. Within these plans, the question that needs to be addressed is what will the guests be feeling at the time of the incident and what can be done to make the best of a bad situation. Service counts even in emergencies.

7
A Glimpse of Tomorrow

The Service Environment

What is ahead for the restaurant industry? Both industry professionals and those considering a career in the industry are asking this question. Although many operations will certainly succeed, analysts' recent predictions for the future of the industry as a whole have been less than optimistic.

Many experts feel that the industry is expanding too rapidly and will probably continue to do so in the future, even though in most markets the number of restaurants already exceeds demand. As one San Francisco analyst predicts, "It is clear that increases in the total number of restaurants have been at an above-average rate at a time when demand has advanced at about an average or normal pace (21). The prospective restaurant glut means that, on average, there will be less traffic per unit and slower sales growth for the industry in general. But, averages do not reveal the true picture, i.e., some restaurants will become more successful at the expense of competitors who will continue to experience sales declines and fail.

Competition from within the restaurant industry is only one challenge facing restaurateurs in the future. Competition is also increasing from supermarkets, convenience food outlets, and other retail stores that sell take-out foods and beverages. For future growth and profitability, restaurants will need to rely on differentiation even more than they did in the past. That differentiation will come, in large part, from service.

Industry Issues and Concerns

Service is not provided in isolation. Managing the guest experience, delivery system techniques, and hospitality are all affected by the larger issues facing the industry. Today's restaurateurs are wrestling with complex issues and concerns that will change the industry's shape. Many of these issues are unique to the industry because of its unparalleled reliance on people to produce unstable and highly personalized products.

Liquor Liability

Liability in serving alcoholic beverages is a critical issue for the restaurant industry today. Alcoholic beverages have been a critical factor in social interaction and industry profitability. In 1984, rising public concern over drunk driving resulted in legislation that cut the federal highway funds of states not in compliance with the 21-year-old drinking age. The legislation has eliminated a vital consumer group for some operators (such as those in college towns) and has caused successful restaurants to fail. Mandatory sentencing for drunk drivers has also affected liquor consumption. This legislation, along with changing consumer behaviors brought about by health and fitness concerns, have resulted in decreased consumption of alcoholic beverages nationwide. This loss of sales and profits has impacted the restaurant industry, which is dependent on both food and beverage income.

Liability Insurance

Third-party liability or "Dram Shop" legislation in many states holds restaurateurs responsible for injuries and deaths caused by intoxicated patrons. "In 35 states, restaurant operators and their employees can be held legally and financially liable for serving a patron who has an accident and injures an innocent third party" (*36*).

The restaurant industry has always opposed drunkenness and intoxicated drivers. However, it questions the rationality of being held liable for personal consumption and behaviors of its guests. Studies support the claim that, "Servers have considerable difficulty in determining whether patrons are intoxicated" (*37*). A recent public relations campaign launched by the American Hotel and Motel Association, called "It's Up To You," emphasizes that moderate alcohol consumption is the responsibility of consumers of alcohol rather than servers of alcohol. The National Restaurant Association states that the majority of consumers support this view. One poll found that "Seventy-two percent of adults believe that bartenders should not be held legally responsible for accidents their customers cause" (*8*).

Increased numbers of liquor and other types of liability suits have made it more expensive or even impossible for some restaurateurs to afford proper insurance coverage. "All over the country people are seeking windfall awards for damages caused by drunk drivers from third parties such as bartenders, restaurant owners, or social hosts. They sue the party most likely to have high liability insurance " (*8*). For many establishments, insurance rates have tripled and sometimes have risen as much as 2000 percent. For others, coverage has been severely cut back or refused entirely.

As in many controversies, there are no easy answers. The restaurant industry has taken responsibility for reducing alcohol abuse and drunk driving with a variety of programs, including eliminating happy hours that feature discounted or promoted beverage alcohol, increasing promotions that emphasize food and non-alcoholic drinks, and providing cab and limousine services for intoxicated customers. Some facilities offer entertainment, such as wide screen televisions, dancing, comedy or magic acts, or live music to deter guests from continuous drinking.

Other companies have instituted alcohol awareness programs for bartenders and servers. These emphasize how to identify intoxication at early stages, responsible service procedures, and how to refuse service. "Manager/owner training focuses on employee practices, attention to marketing strategies which de-emphasize alcohol sales, and changes in the drinking environment to encourage moderate rather than heavy drinking" (*37*).

Responsible facilities are using server training programs such as the National Licensed Beverage Association's Techniques of Alcohol Management (TAM) program. TAM trains servers to rate beverage customers on a three-point scale and serve them accordingly (*30*):

- *Rating number one* applies to guests who have not been drinking. These guests are considered safe to serve.

- *Rating number two* is given to guests who have been drinking, but appear to be in control. Servers need to be alert for signs of intoxication when serving these guests. Many facilities reinforce cautious beverage service with suggestive selling of food and non-alcoholic beverages.

- *Rating number three* applies to intoxicated guests who are no longer in control of themselves and therefore cannot be served. It is often necessary to call a taxi or arrange for a means of safe transportation for these guests.

Other facilities are using blood-alcohol detection devices. One such device "Is a thin plastic tube nearly three inches long. The user breaks a glass vial inside that is filled with yellow crystals and then blows into the tube. If within three minutes the crystals turn completely blue-green, the tester's blood-alcohol content is more than 0.10%, the level considered legally drunk" (*31*) in some states. Some law enforcement officials feel that these devices may do more harm than good; citing that some guests see the devices as a game, and try to see how much they can drink before their blood-alcohol levels register at or above the legal limit.

In the current and foreseeable climate, restaurateurs need to design, implement, and monitor service strategies concerning the responsible sale and service of alcoholic beverages. Selling and serving alcohol responsibly may be one of the most important services a facility provides. As a restaurateur who has a designated driver program in the facility states, "People feel safe here. And if it saves one life, it's worth it" (*14*).

Guest Safety and Health Issues

Many separate issues are having an impact on restaurant safety and sanitation. One serious concern is that of product tampering incidents that have repeatedly surfaced in recent years. Because of the nature of the business, restaurants are vulnerable to food tampering, especially through salad bars, dessert carts, condiment containers, and other areas and items to which the public has access. High employee turnover rates also bring many different employees into contact with food and increase the chances of tampering or food contamination. As one food-service executive warned, "Our industry is a walking time bomb on safety. How many open jars of jelly or other items can you tolerate in a restaurant? We all must take full responsibility for food safety" (28).

The prevention of foodborne illness continues to concern health agencies and food industry leaders. Studies of foodborne illness outbreaks show that foodhandling errors by employees, especially those related to personal hygiene and temperature control, constitute major contributing factors to these outbreaks.

In 1971 the National Conference on Food Protection recommended increased training of foodservice employees as one strategy for raising the level of food safety. Since that time, many training and testing programs, including the Applied Foodservice Sanitation program offered by the Educational Foundation of the National Restaurant Association, have been initiated.

Currently, two states and about 35 local health agencies mandate training and testing of foodservice managers. Many restaurant chains are including manager training and certification as an integral part of their food protection and quality assurance strategies.

One of the most controversial issues in the restaurant industry today is the question of whether or not employees should be tested for Acquired Immune Deficiency Syndrome (AIDS). AIDS, an incurable, fatal disease of the immune system, has alarmed some restaurant guests especially in cities with large incidences of the disease. Restaurant owners, particularly those where there is an emphasis on social interaction, have reported declining sales which they attribute to fear of the AIDS virus.

Some consumer groups are pressuring restaurateurs to test all employees for the disease, but the impact of such testing is hotly debated. Present blood tests for AIDS can only determine whether one has been exposed to the virus, not whether a person has or will contract the disease. Experts agree that AIDS is transmitted primarily through sexual contact, blood transfusions, and shared hypodermic needles.

The National Restaurant Association recently called routine screening for AIDS among food handlers unnecessary and recommended against it. They stated their opposition to screening, "Since any screening of food handlers for AIDS implies that the AIDS virus is passed through casual contact and food, to require screening is to promote panic among the misinformed" (9). Nevertheless, many local restaurant associations feel that some measures must be taken to prevent the public from losing faith in the safety of dining out. Certainly, the future of this issue depends on further research and understanding of the AIDS virus, break-throughs in treatment, and pending state and local legislation regarding food handlers. As AIDS is an extremely complex health problem and social issue, with new developments occurring almost daily, managers have the responsibility to constantly monitor ongoing research and any new governmental regulations. Properly educated personnel is an *absolute* must in this situation.

Product Labeling

Federal legislation requiring ingredient labeling of some menu items is currently under consideration by Congress. This concept, which first appeared in 1979 but failed to generate enough support at that time, resurfaced in 1986 under pressure from a consumer group (The Center for Science in the Public Interest or CSPI). The bill required all chain restaurants with 10 or more units to label food containers in compliance with existing federal label laws for packaged foods sold at the retail level. The group argued that labeling enables consumers who suffer from heart disease to avoid saturated fats, those who have allergies to avoid certain foods or substances, and those who wish to avoid artificial colorings and preservatives to do so. The United States Department of Agriculture (USDA) and the Food and Drug Administration (FDA) rejected the bill stating that the group "Failed to support its claim that 'compelling health reasons' warrant mandatory food ingredient disclosure" and CSPI "Did not demonstrate that new government labeling requirements for 'fast food' would significantly reduce the problems" (*23*).

Although the CSPI bill did not pass, restaurant industry leaders believe labeling will remain an issue and are taking voluntary steps to meet the consumer's need for information.

As of October 1, 1986, fast-service chain companies agreed to disclose nutritional information, including "Calories, protein, carbohydrates, fat, cholesterol, and sodium" (*34*) in consumer brochures rather than on package labels.

Irradiation

Irradiation is a process that exposes food to radiation to kill insects and decay-producing bacteria. Although the process has been approved by the FDA, it has yet to receive final approval from the United States Department of Agriculture (USDA). Irradiation is seen by many as a viable alternative to pesticides and food preservatives.

According to the FDA, if exposed at proper levels, irradiated food is safe for human consumption. The FDA rule allows fruits and vegetables to be exposed to up to 100 kilorads of radiation, and dried spices and vegetables to be exposed to up to 3,000 kilorads.

However, a number of consumer and health groups are very concerned about the use of radiation. Citing a report by the London Food Commission, the Coalition for Alternatives in Nutrition and Healthcare believes that "Any dose [of radiation] can cause the initial damage that develops into a cancer. Polyploidy—a chromosome defect—has been observed in children, monkeys, and rats fed irradiated wheat and hamsters fed an irradiated diet" (18).

Many consumer groups are concerned with a failure by manufacturers and restaurants to declare which foods are irradiated so that consumers who desire to do so can avoid them. Like others in the food industry, restaurateurs are concerned that labeling of irradiated foods would be confusing and upsetting to guests. Currently, the use of low dose radiation is approved for use on fresh pork, dried enzymes, wheat, flour, and fresh produce.

Restaurateurs will need to monitor their guests' opinions on this issue to assess what implications opposition to irradiation has on guest service.

Sulfites

Sulfites, in the form of sulfur dioxide, sodium sulfate, sodium bisulfate, sodium metabisulfate, or potassium metabisulfate, are preservatives used in many packaged foods. They also were used to "Inhibit the growth of bacteria in beer, wine, and ale" (35) and preserve the appearance of fresh produce. Since they "Slow down the browning of fresh fruits and vegetables once they are cut," (35) sulfites were often used in the restaurant industry in fresh fruit salad and salad bars.

Most people have no difficulty tolerating sulfites, but approximately 1 percent of the population (typically those with allergies and some asthmatics) are sensitive to them. Reactions range from mild to fatal and include sneezing, hives, itching, and shock (1, 2).

When these sulfite problems began to surface, many restaurants voluntarily discontinued using sulfites on the foods they prepared. However, restaurants could not control whether or not their suppliers were using them. The new regulations control the use of sulfites by both restaurants and suppliers.

In 1986, the FDA banned the use of sulfites on raw produce (2). "In addition, all packaged foods that contain sulfites, either as a preservative, or as a residue from baking and other processing, must list that ingredient on the label" (2). The FDA also ruled that sulfite warning statements must appear on all alcoholic beverages that contain ten parts-per-million or more of sulfites. This ruling affects most of the wine and some malt beverages sold in the United States. While this ruling (in effect since January 9, 1987) presents a hardship to the wine industry in the way of added expense in printing new wine labels, the Bureau of Alcohol, Tobacco, and Firearms (BATF) has determined that sulfite declaration is necessary (*26*).

Monosodium Glutamate (MSG)

Monosodium glutamate (MSG) is a flavor enhancer used to prepare many kinds of foods. Although MSG may be used in many different kinds of restaurants, its use is associated with Chinese food because it is used to prepare some Oriental dishes. Some people complain of a sensitivity to MSG and report having a "Burning sensation in the neck and forearms, tightness in the chest, and a headache" (*19*) after consuming products prepared with MSG. This response is sometimes called "Chinese Restaurant Syndrome."

New studies indicate that these reactions occur only when MSG is used in "Amounts 'far greater' than those needed for flavor enhancement" (*19*) and that the MSG reactions people report suffering may be symptomatic of more serious illnesses.

Restaurants need to continue devising voluntary programs to provide guests with the health information they require. In this way, they meet consumer needs and address the issues being raised by consumer groups and the government.

Other labeling legislation that is still active concerns hypersensitivity to ingredients. Bills have been presented in Congress to "Mandate ingredient disclosures for restaurant meals in response to the death of a Brown University student who suffered a fatal adverse reaction after eating chili that had been seasoned with peanut butter" (*23*).

A recent FDA advisory committee (The Ad Hoc Advisory Committee on Hypersensitivity to Food Constituents) urged the FDA to "Find a practical means by which complete ingredient information regarding restaurant foods will be conspicuously available at the point of purchase" (*20*). Unlike the recent bill which called for fast food ingredient disclosure, the committee's recommendation called for disclosure of ingredients in all foods in all types of establishments.

Guest confidence in restaurants increases when guests believe the industry is doing all in its power to protect their health and well-being. Ingredient labeling may help accomplish this guest confidence and contribute to value-added service.

Smoking/Non-smoking Seating Sections

At present, 12 states and 80 different counties mandate that restaurants offer non-smoking sections to guests. While restaurant owners agree that many guests find cigarette smoke disturbing when dining out, some still oppose legislation that forces them to provide non-smoking sections. Current legislation in effect in some areas requires restaurateurs to set aside a certain percentage of their seating for non-smokers regardless of guest demand.

Smoking and non-smoking sections put managers in a position to enforce the policy, thereby creating the risk that they will create ill will among their guests. Thus, one of the most important guest relations function is to develop a procedure to deal with the enforcement of smoking or non-smoking sections. For example, once a non-smoking section of a restaurant has been designated:

- Sign it clearly.

- Remove ash trays from the tables.

- Have the host offer the option of smoking or non-smoking sections during the seating procedure.

- When either section is filled and the other is open, guests should be given the option to sit in the open section rather than wait for a table.

- Guests should never have to enforce the policy through complaints to management.

- Enforcement is the responsibility of the manager, not the servers. Servers should report to the manager when a guest smokes in a non-smoking section.

- When managers approach guests who are smoking in a non-smoking area, they should:

  Be discreet, talk quietly, and assume it was the restaurant's fault in not making the policy clear to the guests.

  Apologize for the request to extinguish the cigarette, cigar, or pipe, but be clear that no smoking is permitted in the section.

  Offer to move guests to a table in the smoking section when one is available.

  When the option is chosen, help guests move to the new table.

Always thank guests twice for cooperating, first right after the incident, and again when they leave the facility.

Business Meal Tax Deductions

In June, 1986, the United States Senate passed the final version of a tax reform bill that cut the deductibility of business meals by 20 percent. The 80 percent meal tax cap, designed to help trim the United States Treasury deficit, was passed.

The National Restaurant Association intends to monitor the impact of the bill on the industry and, if necessary, lobby to reverse the deductibility cutbacks already in effect and prevent any further cuts. Meanwhile, restaurants can serve guests by providing completed guest receipts and using charge forms that make it easier for guests to comply with the recordkeeping requirements of the new law.

Labor Issues

The restaurant industry, which is labor-intensive, is greatly concerned about several labor issues. A steep increase in the federal minimum wage has been proposed in several recent bills. This legislation, if enacted, will add hundreds of millions of dollars to foodservice labor costs.

An immigration reform bill passed in November, 1986, subjects restaurateurs to stiff penalties for hiring illegal aliens. "Key provisions of the new law leave employers vulnerable to fines of up to $2,000 for each illegal alien found on the payroll. Repeat offenders face even harsher sanctions, including fines up to $10,000 per undocumented worker and six-month prison terms" (27). Under the law, as of June 1, 1987, employers will be required to verify the immigration status of all new employees and complete and keep detailed documents establishing legal residency.

Employee meals is another area of concern. Many workers receive employer-subsidized meals in company cafeterias and dining rooms. The Internal Revenue Service (IRS) is now seeking to require that workers pay income taxes on the value of these meals. If this measure passes, labor relations problems may occur in the industry since many workers will resent being taxed for meals they may not have eaten.

The restaurant industry is concerned about other proposed labor legislation including: restricting restaurants from requiring employees to submit to polygraph (lie detector) tests; raising the minimum salary by which assistant managers and other supervisors are exempt from overtime pay requirements; and changing child labor laws regarding job duties that may be performed by minors in restaurants. Restaurateurs feel that further restrictions may increase the labor shortage that many facilities are already experiencing.

Reservation Policy and No-Shows

Some restaurateurs provide guests the opportunity to reserve tables for specific dates and times. This guest service is frequently demanded by guests, but not always understood. A perspective that may help clarify the issue is that restaurateurs are in the business of renting chairs in the dining room. When a guest requests that a table be set aside and the restaurateur complies, there is an implied contract between the two parties to perform. No major problem exists during slow periods, but this service policy can become costly and a serious point of difference on the part of both parties during peak periods.

Swings in guest traffic are common to the industry. Some special occasion restaurants account for 25 to 30 percent of their weekly guest traffic and sales on one evening and up to 70 percent over three days. In other words, table turnover becomes more critical to a restaurant's economic survival at certain times. It is usually at these times that reservations are requested by guests.

Needless to say, a table for four being unemployed during periods of high guest demand is costly. For example, a restaurant with an average guest check of $20.00 and an average table turnover time of 90 minutes is paying over $.22 cents a minute a chair or losing sales of close to $.90 per minute for each minute the party is late.

Formulating an effective policy for dealing with late reservations and no-shows (people who make reservations but do not honor them) is a critical management decision. It is a point of great debate among restaurateurs. The problem, once unique to the United States and now cropping up in Europe, severely cuts into restaurant profits. In some restaurants, the no-show rate is as high as 50 percent. It is especially prevalent in fine-dining restaurants and in larger cities where people often make reservations at several restaurants and then decide at the last minute where they will dine.

In an effort to cut down on the number of late parties and no-shows, restaurateurs are using different strategies with varying degrees of success. These include:

- Explaining that the party will be seated as close to the desired time as possible, rather than quoting a guaranteed time of seating.

- Requiring guests to reconfirm their reservations.

- Keeping a computerized check list of no-shows. When previous no-shows call to make a reservation, they are reminded to call and cancel their reservations if their plans change. If they appear on the no-show list a second time, their reservations are not accepted.

- Overbooking reservations, especially during late hours of operation (a dangerous practice and one that will surely create strained guest relations at times). When employing this practice, management must also have a policy for managing guests who arrive only to find no space available for a lengthy period.

- Shortening the time for which reservations will be held to five or ten minutes. However, this also implies the guest will not have to wait for a table longer than ten minutes.

- Requiring non-refundable credit card deposits, especially for weekend, holiday, and large party reservations. But, restaurateurs should be prepared to lose loyal guests when this policy is enforced.

- Some restaurants find that a "No Reservations" policy works best and seat guests on a first-come, first-served basis. Others accept reservations on certain days, but not on others. If these policies are enacted, some options for consideration are:

  Make certain the policy is made clear to guests.

  Be sure the wait for dinner is enjoyable. Comfortable and well-designed space should be available for parties who want beverage alcohol and those who do not.

  Give guests something enjoyable to do while they wait. Entertainment, conversation pieces (art, antiques, memorabilia, etc.), tours, and garden walks are all used successfully.

  Provide some special food to eat while waiting.

  Make certain the communication system used is effective in letting guests know their tables are ready. However, the system should not be annoying to guests.

  Have V.I.P. service for regulars (those special guests who frequent the facility). This may include a special lounge for waiting and drinking. However, such a policy must not be mismanaged and slight other patrons.

Managers have to balance the benefits of stringent no-show policies and procedures with the extent to which they antagonize loyal guests or make them think twice before making a reservation. Some guests do not keep reservations or are late for valid reasons, such as family emergencies and traffic tie-ups. If a facility applies no-show policies to individuals inappropriately, it is sure to lose valuable guests.

New Service Demands

"Success depends on identifying and meeting changing customer needs" (*24*) was the prevailing message at a recent industry conference. Changing consumer needs and new market segments have brought about new service demands throughout the industry and will continue to do so in the future.

Whatever their age, income, marital status, or health consciousness, it can be said that consumers today are more sophisticated when it comes to dining out. They are not fooled by dressed-up poor quality food or fancy restaurants with poor service. They no longer allow themselves to be intimidated into accepting poor treatment from fine-dining establishments. Instead, poor service wastes their time and makes them angry.

In general, today's consumers have many alternatives to eating out in restaurants and are more demanding in terms of restaurant quality, price/value benefit, and product information. They are also more experimental and see dining out as an opportunity for new experiences. New foods and new service options appeal to them. Consumers are overwhelmed with choices available in the present marketplace and their lifestyles and tastes are shifting. Successful restaurateurs use all available resources to keep pace with their changing needs and new market segments.

Creativity and Innovation

Restaurant success is, and always will be, based on creativity and innovation. In an industry where competition is the byword, creativity and innovation are absolute necessities. A senior vice-president for a large pizza chain advises, "You must understand what is driving your business. Using convenience as an example of a major force driving the business today, it is possible to mesh the consumer's need for convenience with the company's requirement for penetration. Can increasing penetration go on forever? Of course not, especially if you define location in the traditional context of a free-standing unit. You have to let your mind go. You can access more customers through delivery. You can build mini-units in malls or airports, or on military bases, etc. You cannot lock yourself into a set format" (*31*).

New concepts in the industry quickly become old hat. Experts agree that continuous innovation in the industry can keep businesses going and can help prevent guests from satisfying their appetites elsewhere—namely convenience stores, supermarkets, and upscale take-out shops.

Unfortunately, there is often so much time-consuming research and development required before implementing a new idea, that the idea is old before it ever becomes a reality. This results in a boring operation, out of step with its guests' needs. Although restaurateurs should be cautious when developing new ideas, they do need to recognize that timing is a primary consideration.

A prominent trade publisher advises against innovation without good reason. "This is a sure way to get nowhere. When you alter the things that made you successful and you become unrecognizable and confusing to your tried and true loyal customers, they're going to go someplace else because they have a myriad of choices" (*10*).

Successful restaurateurs say that serving food is really a fashion business. Nothing remains constant. New concepts come along quickly, get rave reviews, and die just as quickly. The "big idea" or successful new restaurant concept can be identified using the following criteria (*4*):

- Lines of people of varied descriptions (age, income, and so forth) are waiting to eat while other nearby restaurants have no waiting lines.

- After you have eaten, you have a pressing urge to share your discovered experience with all your friends.

- You have difficulty in clearly describing it. (It's not exactly like anything else, therefore, no one has found precise language to define it.)

- You wish you had thought of the idea and opened the restaurant yourself.

- Within six months the trade press has picked up on it, and other operators are cloning it—but often without the same success.

- It has long-term viability.

Why are creativity and innovation especially important at this time in the restaurant industry? The large number of consumers, now in the 30- to 60-year-old age group, who will set the trends for the industry in the coming years are in search of new experiences. Because they are sophisticated and have discretionary income, they seek a new, different, and exciting experience. Restaurants that can provide such an experience by being creative and innovative will reap the rewards.

Restaurateurs are taking a fresh look at traditional service problems and formulating some creative solutions. For example, a combination laundromat and upscale cafe in Austin, Texas, has answered the consumer problem of what to do while your clothes are washing and drying at the laundromat. This successful establishment, located near apartment complexes and the University of Texas, allows students and others to sample a variety of imported Italian deli offerings while they take care of one of life's chores (5). Also, burger buses (mobile fast-service restaurants) were introduced by one fast-service company in 1985. They allow the company to enter new markets that were once unfeasible, such as military bases, health-care facilities, colleges and universities, seasonal resorts, and long-term construction projects, with a minimum of energy, operational, and labor costs.

Delivery

Food delivery services are increasing in various parts of the country. Creatively designed, home or office delivery offers restaurateurs new sources of profit, but it is not without new problems. The problems with delivery include maintaining product quality during travel time, the difficulties of delivering over distances, the additional cost of inefficient service, marketing larger menus, communications systems, and insurance and automobile costs.

One leader in home-delivery of pizza, with a reputation for guest satisfaction, explains the company's success in a recent article on the at-home market, "One of the big factors in our success is that we have kept the menu simple. We offer pizza and only one beverage. That way, we are able to focus on one concept: delivering our product within 30 minutes" (32). The company uses high technology and high efficiency to keep its promise to guests of pizza in 30 minutes. The company states, "We've got it down to 60 seconds from order to oven, and every step of the way, we pride ourselves on an in-store urgency to get that pizza delivered within the promised time" (32). The company is also experimenting with a central ordering system in which consumers would call a central number and a computer would route the order to the unit nearest the guest's home.

This company and others are also experimenting with mobile cooking units designed to speed up delivery to homes and to set up shop in temporary sites such as fairs and construction sites. One Indiana-based pizza chain is using radio-dispatched trucks that carry a pizza inventory. This speeds delivery by eliminating yet another step in the restaurant-to-guest service process.

In the past, home delivery was generally limited to pizza (and ice cream if you count early ice cream trucks) and a few other individualized restaurants; however, that too is changing. Home delivery is now being tested for Chinese food, chicken, ribs, Mexican food, and even hamburgers. A new company in Austin, Texas, delivers full course meals (from five of the city's best restaurants) in less than 45 minutes. Guests can also order wine, beer, or videocassettes to accompany their food. The company's business is booming and its gross sales will reach $1 million in the company's first year of operation.

Other businesses are also mixing food offerings with entertainment in a home-delivery package. Two Chicago area establishments and a Detroit restaurant are offering food, videocassettes, or both. Video deliveries now make up about 40 percent of one of the restaurant's business. These restaurants offer free pick up of the videocassette the next day—the ultimate guest convenience.

Home delivery of food and videocassettes seems to be an innovation guaranteed to succeed. Today, 29 percent of all American households have VCRs. Analysts predict that by 1990, 70 percent of households—a total of 70 million—will own them (*31*). The development of more food and video delivery services is expected to parallel the boom in VCR ownership.

Additionally, home-delivery operations are extremely profitable. "Costs of installation, operation, and labor are reduced in comparison with units specializing in on-premise dining, thereby increasing profit margins. Space requirements for a dedicated home-delivery unit are half of those for an eat-in establishment, while total fixed investment is drastically reduced (for facilities and equipment) and return on investment is two to three times as high for the dedicated unit" (*31*).

Service Is the Future

Most industry experts see personalized service as the secret ingredient to a successful restaurant industry in the years ahead. One fast-service company executive believes in improving service and concentrating on

"Human resources rather than capital resources ... We've got to put the 'quick' back in quick service" (*21*).

At a recent industry conference, analysts and restaurateurs agreed that many in the industry have forgotten about the basic qualities of service, with disastrous results. Most industry experts see improved service as the secret weapon in dealing with the unstable immediate future of the industry.

Successful restaurateurs know that while service design and operations are extremely important, the real force behind good service is employees. "It is the person out there on the front-lines dealing with customers [one at a time] day-to-day who represents your company [and it is the employees'] interaction with the customers and how their performances are perceived by the customers that make the difference. All the great intentions of the home office don't add up to much if your employees are ill-suited" (*31*). Restaurant managers believe that motivating and communicating with employees are key elements in offering excellent service.

Excellent service is an ingredient that is sorely missing in many of today's restaurants. One industry consultant told attendees at an industry conference that it's time to bring back quality service. "With the sophistication and coming of age of the restaurant industry in recent years, the primary emphasis has increasingly shifted toward food and away from the customer. The quality of service has suffered as a result" (*22*).

The consultant blames both a lack of discipline on management's part and a lack of consistent standards for declining service. "The lack of customer focus is ridiculous. About 65 percent of the people who serve food don't give a damn if it satisfies the customer. The number one priority when we have standards is to identify and satisfy customer needs profitably" (*22*). To improve the quality of service, restaurants need to "Regard serving food as a mission to create a pleasant dining experience for every person who eats in the restaurant" (*22*).

All indicators point to quality service as the driving force in the future of the restaurant industry. Service is what guests want and the success of today's and tomorrow's restaurants depends upon their ability to provide it.

References

CHAPTER 1

TEXTBOOKS

1. **In Search of Excellence: Lessons from America's Best-run Companies**
   Thomas J. Peters and Robert H. Waterman. Jr.
   Harper & Row Publishers, 1982

2. **The Marketing Imagination**
   Theodore Levitt
   The Free Press
   A Division of Macmillan, Inc., 1983

3. **Megatrends: Ten New Directions Transforming Our Lives**
   John Naisbitt
   Warner Books, Inc.
   A Warner Communications Company, 1982, 1984

4. **The Reckoning: The Challenge to America's Greatness**
   David Halberstam
   William Morrow, 1986

5. **Service America: Doing Business in the New Economy**
   Karl Albrecht and Ron Zemke
   Dow Jones-Irwin, 1985

TRADE AND INDUSTRY PUBLICATIONS

Advertising Age

April 11, 1985

6. "Restaurants Feast on Menu Diversity, Growth"
   Peter Francese

Frozen Food Age

March 1986

7. "Who Eats Where, Why and When is Subject of Study by NRA"

Nation's Restaurant News

February 4, 1985

8. "Marketing for Mature Americans"
   Howard Riell

9. "Operators Face Price Dilemma"
   Rick Telberg

10. "Senior Citizens—Food Service's Untapped Market"

September 23, 1985

11. "More Operators Turn to Takeout"
    Don Jeffrey

September 30, 1985

12. "What Do Customers Want? Independents Grapple with Changing Tastes in Food"
    Paul Frumkin

November 25, 1985

13. "Forecast: Convenience Foods will Post Biggest Gains in '86"
    Joe Edwards

March 10, 1986

14. "Fast Feeders are Major Winners in Take-out Sweepstakes"
    Don Jeffrey

15. "Viewpoint: Here Comes the Shakeout"
    Charles S. Glovsky and Steven A. Rockwell

April 14, 1986

16. "Ethnic Foods: What American Consumers Want"
    Peter Romeo

April 28, 1986

17. "Going the Distance with Home Delivery"
    Don Jeffrey

May 12, 1986

18. "Gallup Eating-out Survey Offers Special Psychographic Analysis"
    David Zuckerman

19. "Survey Offers Good News, Bad News: USDA Poll Shows American Diners Getting Older—but Richer"

May 19, 1986

20. "Gallup Poll: Eating-Out Pace Flat for Second Year"

June 9, 1986

21. "Patrons Seek Healthier Foods: NRA Survey Suggests New Marketing Tacks"
    Rick Telberg

July 14, 1986

22. "Gallup Survey: Nutrition Plays Strong Role in Dining Decisions"

September 22, 1986

23. "IFMA Forecasts Slowdown in '87: 1.6% Growth Rate Predicted"
    Rick Telberg

January 1, 1987

24. "Forecasters Paint Grey Picture for 1987"

Restaurant Business

June 10, 1986

25. "Tapping the At-home Market"
    Sarah Person

The Wall Street Journal

April 21, 1986

26. "Dining Chic to Chic"

OTHER MATERIALS

27. **The 1985 / 86 Gallup Annual Report on Eating Out**
    The Gallup Organization, Inc.
    Princeton, New Jersey, 1986

28. **Training For Hospitality**
    Dr. Lewis C. Forrest, Jr.
    National Restaurant Association

CHAPTER 2

TEXTBOOKS

1. **Food and People**
    Third Edition
    Miriam E. Lowenberg, E. Neige Todhunter, Eva D. Wilson, Jane R. Savage, and James L. Lubawski
    John Wiley & Sons, Inc., 1979

2. **Introduction to Hotel and Restaurant Management, A Book of Readings**
    Third Edition
    Edited by Robert A. Brymer
    Kendall/Hunt Publishing Co., 1981

3. **Marketing Principles: The Management Process**
    Ben Enis
    Goodyear Publishing Co., 1974
    as quoted in (2) above

TRADE AND INDUSTRY PUBLICATIONS

Candy Marketer

July/August, 1986

4. "Chips and Chunks"

Nation's Restaurant News

July 16, 1984

5. "Twenty-five Years: The Four Seasons Basking in the Summer of its First
    100 Seasons"
    Paul Frumkin

October 15, 1984

6. "Chocolate: The New After-dinner 'Mint' "
    Marilee Hartley

December 3, 1984

7. "Ad/Promo Perspective: Why Put Your Money Where Your Word-of-
    Mouth is?"
    Ken Frydman

December 17, 1984

8. "Marketing Plan Designed to Cater to College Crowds"

January 2, 1985

9. "Ad/Promo Perspective: Two Restaurants Break all Rules' and Bring in
    Traffic"
    Ken Frydman

January 7, 1985

10. "Food Industry is Overlooking the Importance of Advertising"
    Ken Frydman

March 18, 1985

11. "Forge, General Store: Dual-concept Dining"
NRN West Coast Bureau

July 15, 1985

12. "Extensive Wine List Educates Customers at Salishan Lodge"
Mort Hochstein

July 22, 1985

13. "Starker's Gets Customers Involved in Wine Selection"
Patt Paterson

August 12, 1985

14. "Spats Changes Style for 'Maturing' Clientele"

September 30, 1985

15. "Star Clipper: An Elegant Restaurant on Wheels"
Howard Riell

October 7, 1985

16. "Yuppies 'Network' at N.Y. Restaurants"
Ken Frydman

March 17, 1986

17. "Turning Slow Time into Tea Time"
Peter Romeo

April 7, 1986

18. "Patrons Help Solve 'Murder Mystery' "
Alan Liddle

May 12, 1986

19. "Coco Palms' Flame Room Doesn't Resort to Menu"

Restaurant Business

May 1, 1986

20. "Know your Niche"
Peter Berlinski

Restaurants & Institutions

February 5, 1986

21. "What's in it for you: Catering to the Junior and Senior Customers"

August 20, 1986

22. "The Sky's the Limit"
Elizabeth Faulkner, Jeffrey Weinstein, Howard Schlossberg, and Laura Pokrzywa

November 12, 1986

23. "Redesigned Menu Offers Something for Everyone"
    Kathleen Marshall

OTHER MATERIALS

24. **Managing Word-Of-Mouth Promotion**
    Donald I. Smith
    Manuscript Draft, 11/13/85

CHAPTER 3

TEXTBOOKS

1. **The Complete Manager**
   Edward M. Harwell
   Lebhar-Friedman Books
   Chain Store Publishing Corp., 1985

2. **Customer Relations**
   Third Edition
   Lloyd W. Moseley
   Lebhar-Friedman Books
   Chain Store Publishing Corp., 1983

3. **Introduction to Hotel and Restaurant Management, A Book of Readings**
   Third Edition
   Edited by Robert A. Brymer
   Kendall/Hunt Publishing Co., 1981

4. **Managing People: Techniques For Food Service Operators**
   Neil R. Sweeney
   Lebhar-Friedman Books
   Chain Store Publishing Corp., 1986

5. **Managing Restaurant Personnel: A Handbook for Food Service Operators**
   John R. Bryan
   Chain Store Age Books
   Chain Store Publishing Corp., 1974

6. **Managing and Training People**
   Edward M. Harwell
   Lebhar-Friedman Books
   Chain Store Publishing Corp., 1983

7. **Service America: Doing Business in the New Economy**
Karl Albrecht and Ron Zemke
Dow Jones-Irwin, 1985

TRADE AND INDUSTRY PUBLICATIONS

IGA Grocergram
September, 1986

8. "Evaluating Employee Performance—Ten Errors to Avoid"
Kay Melchisedech Olson

Marketing News
June 21, 1985

9. "Staffing is Key to Success in the Hospitality Industry"

Nation's Restaurant News
November 26, 1984

10. "Zraly Tells Wine Seminar: Staff Training is Paramount"

December 3, 1984

11. "Viewpoint: Smoking—Walking the Tightrope Between Demands and Duties"
Stanley R. Kyker

December 17, 1984

12. "Six Ways to Keep Hourly Employees on the Job"
Robert J. Harloe

February 4, 1985

13. "Corporate Values Determine the Success of Training"
John L. Avella

March 11, 1985

14. "Long Waits can Ruin a First Impression"
Richard J. Pezzullo

June 3, 1985

15. "Seminar Focuses on Best Way to Provide On-the-job Training"

16. "Thelander Offers Formula for Finding Top Employees"

June 10, 1985

17. "Clinic Stresses Employee Motivation as Key"
Alan Liddle

August 19, 1985

18. "Beyond Traditional Recruiting: 9 Ways to Hire"
Robert J. Harloe

19. "Lebhar-Friedman Research"

20. "Staff Deserves Personal Touch"
Letter: Dean M. Corcoran

September 2, 1985

21. "McD Tries Recruiting Customers"

November 18, 1985

22. "Service with a Smile: Practicing 'Uncommon' Courtesy Makes Good
Dollars and Sense"
Dan Flora and Andy Elkind

June 23, 1986

23. "Restaurant Execs Share Insights at SFM Conference"
NRN Midwest Bureau

July 28, 1986

24. "Viewpoint: Chain of Command is Right On"
Letter: C. Vincent Shortt

September 22, 1986

25. "How One Chain Combats the Dwindling Teenage Work Force"
David Zuckerman

New York Times

September 4, 1986

26. "As Service Standards Decline, a Few Restaurants Still Excel"
Bryan Miller

Restaurants & Institutions

May 28, 1986

27. "1986 JOB$ Survey Results: Money, Ambition Drive Youthful Foodser-
vice Pros"
Jane Grant Tougas

September 3, 1986

28. "Hospitality Education a Growth Industry, NIFI Directories Show"

October 1, 1986

29. "Fast-Food Operators Report Most Labor Problems"
Jeff Weinstein

OTHER MATERIALS

30. **The Golden Corral CARE Program**
    General Instructions Manual
    Golden Corral, 1984

31. **Waitress—Order of Service**
    Mr. Steak, Inc., 1979

32. **NRA Project Hospitality**
    Advisory Committee Meeting Notes
    Sandy Corporation, August 16, 1981

33. **Training for Hospitality**
    Dr. Lewis C. Forrest, Jr.
    National Restaurant Association

CHAPTER 4

TEXTBOOKS

1. **Food Service Management**
   Third Edition
   Charles E. Eshbach
   CBI Publishing Company, Inc., 1979

2. **Practical Guide to Customer Service Management and Operations**
   E. Patricia Birsner and Ronald D. Balsley
   AMACOM - A Division of American Management Associations, 1982

3. **Profitable Food and Beverage Management: Operations**
   Eric F. Green, Galen G. Drake, and F. Jerome Sweeney
   Hayden Book Company, Inc., 1978

TRADE AND INDUSTRY PUBLICATIONS

Nation's Restaurant News

September 30, 1985

4. "Members Protest Smoking Curb"
   Marilyn Alva

December 16, 1985

5. " 'Burger Buses' Could Revolutionize the Industry"

February 17, 1986

6. "Spiaggia's Private Dining Rooms Exceed Anticipation"
   Carolyn Walkup

February 24, 1986

7. "Viewpoint: A Matter of Choice: Profits Go Up in Smoke when Non-smoking Sections are Mandatory"
Jean E. Palmieri

March 10, 1986

8. "Second-tier Chains: Small Cafeterias Conservative in Growth Plans"
Mark Schoifet

April 7, 1986

9. "Two Views on Smoking Issue"
Letters: Mike McConnell, James H. Ammon

July 7, 1986

10. "KFC Cuts Serving Time 20 Percent"
Ken Frydman

October 6, 1986

11. "Little King Testing New Delivery 'Van'"

October 27, 1986

12. "Quik Wok Tests Take-out and Delivery"
Richard Martin

November 17, 1986

13. "New Headset a Boon for Drive-thrus"
Rick Van Warner

OTHER MATERIALS

14. **The 1985/86 Gallup Annual Report on Eating Out**
The Gallup Organization, Inc.
Princeton, New Jersey, 1986

15. **Customer Quality Expectations: The Saga Difference**
Education Division Quality Standards
SAGA Corporation

CHAPTER 5

TEXTBOOKS

1. **Service America: Doing Business in the New Economy**
Karl Albrecht and Ron Zemke
Dow Jones-Irwin, 1985

TRADE AND INDUSTRY PUBLICATIONS

Canadian Hotel & Restaurant

2. January, 1985
    "Birthday Promotions: Bright Ideas for New Business"
    Bob McClelland

Nation's Restaurant News

September 24, 1984

3. "Cypress Matching Customers to their Dishes"

October 15, 1984

4. "Chocolate: The New After-dinner 'Mint' "
    Marilee Hartley

November 5, 1984

5. "Hotels See Fit to Shape Up Menus"
    Paul Frumkin

December 3, 1984

6. "Currents in Cuisine: Keep Complimentary Treats Worthy of Compliments"
    Florence Fabricant

January 2, 1985

7. "Using Bread to Create a Good First Impression"
    Susan Spedalle

February 25, 1985

8. "Very Few Restaurants Listening to the Needs of Deaf Customers"
    Alan Liddle

May 6, 1985

9. "Lang's Vision Brings Life to 60-Year-Old Restaurant"

May 20, 1985

10. "Making Customers Feel Special Boosts Business"
    Sarah Shankman

June 24, 1985

11. "Ritz-Carlton Children's Menu a Coloring Book"

July 15, 1985

12. "McD Adds Flair to its Breakfast"
    David Zuckerman

July 22, 1985

13. "Reporter's Journal: Celebrating Grandparents"
    Joe Edwards

August 19, 1985

14. "Operators Add Catering: Sage, Errant Tap Source of Extra Sales"
    Carolyn Walkup

October 21, 1985

15. "Chicago Hilton Completes Renovations"
    Carolyn Walkup

November 18, 1985

16. ' "Thoughtful Touches': Ponder's Way"
    Richard Martin

March 10, 1986

17. "Just Desserts"
    Marilyn Alva

April 7, 1986

18. "Canadians Spending More on Meals in U.S. than any Other Foreign
    Tourists"
    NRN Washington Bureau

April 14, 1986

19. "USTTA Promotes American Food to Foreign Tourists"
    NRN Washington Bureau

April 28, 1986

20. "Operators Court Single Consumers: Independent Restaurateurs Redis-
    cover Counter Service"
    Richard Martin

June 16, 1986

21. "McDonald's Speaks Loud and Clear with 'Silent Persuasion'"
    David Zuckerman

June 23, 1986

22. "Elegance Out, 'Food-sharing' In at Dallas Lincoln's Restaurant"
    Marilyn Alva

October 27, 1986

23. "Chi-Chi's Franchise Group to Women: Let's Have Lunch"
    Marilyn Alva

New York Magazine

November 3, 1986

24. "Power House: How the Four Seasons Does It"
Peter Hellman

Restaurant Business

May 6, 1986

25. "Niche Marketing"
Denise M. Brennan

Restaurants & Institutions

February 5, 1986

26. "What's in it for You: Catering to the Junior and Senior Customers"

August 20, 1986

27. "The Sky's the Limit"
Elizabeth Faulkner, Jeffrey Weinstein, Howard Schlossberg, and Laura Pokrzywa

September 3, 1986

28. ' "America's Business Breakfast' Served at Selected Hiltons"

September 17, 1986

29. "News to Make Hearts Happy"
Julie Mautner

October 29, 1986

30. "Cooking for Kids"
Lorry Zirlin

CHAPTER 6

TEXTBOOKS

1. **Chain Drug Store Management and Operations**
Robert J. Bolger, Sc.D. and Jude P. West, Ph.D.
Cornell University, 1984

2. **Introduction to Hotel and Restaurant Management, A Book of Readings**
Third Edition
Edited by Robert A. Brymer
Kendall/Hunt Publishing Co., 1981

3. **Practical Guide to Customer Service Management and Operations**
   E. Patricia Birsner and Ronald D. Balsley
   AMACOM - A Division of American Management Associations, 1982

TRADE AND INDUSTRY PUBLICATIONS

Candy Marketer

July / August, 1986

4. "Chips and Chunks"

Progressive Grocer

October, 1985

5. "Violent Crime Dealing with a Deadly Issue"
   Michael Sansolo

OTHER MATERIALS

6. **The Handbook of Basic Managerial Communication**
   Water D. St. John
   Human Resources Development Department
   Friendly Ice Cream Corp., May 15, 1984

7. **Loss Prevention Handbook**
   SAGA Corporation

CHAPTER 7

TRADE AND INDUSTRY PUBLICATIONS

FDA Consumer

June 1986
Volume 20, Number 5

1. "Food Allergies: Separating Fact from 'Hype' "
   Richard C. Thompson

February, 1987
Volume 21, Number 1

2. "Rx Drugs to Carry Sulfite Warning"

Market Watch

April 1985

3. "Goodbye Happy Hour"
   Suzanne Rella

Nation's Restaurant News

December 3, 1984

4. "Viewpoint: Smoking—Walking the Tightrope Between Demands and Duties"
   Stanley R. Kyker

April 29, 1985

5. "Singles Swing to New Food-service Beat: The Barwash: Food and Suds"
   Marilyn Alva

July 8, 1985

6. "Labeling Plan Resurfaces, Chains Face Ingredient Disclosure Rules"
   Ken Rankin

7. "Dateline D.C. Sanitation Test Could Dispose of Jobs"
   Ken Rankin

July 15, 1985

8. "Inside Washington Survey: Dram Shop is Out of Step"
   Ken Rankin

October 28, 1985

9. "Presidents Debate Impact of Testing Employees for AIDS"

November 14, 1985

10. "MUFSO Report Anderman: Competition Leads to Innovation"
    Mark Schoifet

December 16, 1985

11. "Viewpoint: The Big Idea—Developing an Original Concept is Difficult but not Impossible"
    Donald I. Smith

February 17, 1986

12. "Viewpoint: An Attitude Adjustment, The Time has Come to Condemn Abusers of the Liability System"
    Joe R. Lee

February 24, 1986

13. "Viewpoint: A Matter of Choice, Profits Go Up in Smoke when Non-smoking Sections are Mandatory"
    Jean E. Palmieri

March 24, 1986
NRN Bar Management Supplement

14. "Designated-driver Programs Gain Greater Acceptance: Encouraging Patrons to Shun Alcohol is Helping to Lessen Server Responsibility and Lower Insurance Costs"

April 28, 1986

15. "Viewpoint: Latest Analysis Reveals Proposed Meal Cap Worse than Thought"
Ken Rankin

May 19, 1986

16. "No Traffic-count Rebound in Sight for 1986, Expert Says"
Rick Telberg

July 21, 1986

17. "New Devices Aid DWI Battle: Restaurateur Tries Out Blood-alcohol Tester"
Ken Frydman

September 8, 1986

18. "Health Group: Irradiation is Food Roulette, Cites Findings of New British Study"

19. "Recent Study Claims MSG has Bum Rap"
NRN Washington Bureau

September 15, 1986

20. "FDA Committee Urges 'Complete' Labeling Decision: Panel Recommends Finding Practical Means for Display"

October 6, 1986

21. "MUFSO '86: The Future is Now—Analysts, Chain Leaders Paint Bleak Portrait of '87"

22. "Beveridge Stresses Standards, Stronger Focus on Customers"

23. "Mandatory Labeling Advocates Losing Ground in Washington"
Ken Rankin

24. "MUFSO '86: The Future is Now—Multi-concept Panel: Identifying, Meeting Needs the Key to Success"

October 27, 1986

25. "New Legislation Makes it Easier to Counter Rising Premiums"
Ken Rankin

26. "Sulfite Labeling to Appear on Alcoholic Beverages: Rule Mandates Warning on 'All but a Few' Wines"
NRN Washington Bureau

November 3, 1986

27. "Immigration Bill Offers Paperwork and Penalties"
    Ken Rankin
28. "Quaker Oats Executive Warns of Safety 'Time Bomb': Jones Addresses
    Fall Management Conference"
    Charles Bernstein

November 17, 1986
29. "FDA Plans to Recommend Food-service Operator Certification"

March 30, 1987
Bar Management Supplement
30. "The Role Bartenders Play in Positive Drinking"

Restaurant Business

May 6, 1986
31. "Niche Marketing"
    Denise M. Brennan

June 10, 1986
32. "Tapping the At-home Market"
    Sarah Person

Restaurant Hospitality

April, 1986
33. "Foodborne Illness Worries FDA"
    Tony Glaros

Restaurants & Institutions

October 29, 1986
34. "Labeling Issue Moves to States: California, Texas Work Together—Cut
    Deals with Fast-food Chains"

Tufts University Diet & Nutrition Letter

December, 1984
Volume 2, Number 10
35. "More Warnings on Sulfites"

OTHER MATERIALS

36. **The Beverage Alcohol Market, Wine & Spirits Market . . . Past, Present,
    Future**
    National Account Sales
    Joseph E. Seagram & Sons, Inc., 1985–86

37. **Legal Liabilities of Licensed Alcoholic Beverage Establishments: Recent Developments in the United States**
    James F. Mosher, J.D.
    Prevention Research Center, Revised, June, 1984

Appendix:
Newspapers, Periodicals, and other Service-Related Information Sources

Advertising Age
Circulation Department
965 East Jefferson
Detroit, Michigan 48207
(312) 446-0494

American Automatic Merchandiser
P.O. Box 6310
Duluth, Minnesota 55806-9964
(218) 723-9200

Amusement Business
Griener Customer Service
P.O. Box 2072
Mahopac, New York 10541-9954
(914) 628-7771

Bakery Production and Marketing
8750 West Bryn Mawr Avenue
Chicago, Illinois 60631
(312) 693-3200

Barron's
300 North Zeeb Road
Ann Arbor, Michigan 48106
(800) 521-0600

Between the Lines / Washington Spectator
P.O. Box 442
Merrifield, Virginia 22116
(703) 691-1271

Briefing
1001 Kings Avenue, #201
Jacksonville, Florida 32207-8311
(904) 396-3052

Business Week
Princeton Hightstown Road
Hightstown, New Jersey 08520
(609) 426-7500

Cameron's Foodservice Promotions Reporter
P.O. Box 1160, 5325 Sheridan Drive
Williamsville, New York 14221
(716) 834-4159

Canadian Hotel and Restaurant
Maclean Hunter Ltd.
777 Bay Street
Toronto, Ontario M5W 1A7, Canada
(416) 596-5782

Chain Marketing and Management
Cahner's Publishing Company
44 Cook Street
Denver, Colorado 80206
(303) 388-4511

Chain Store Age
305 Madison Avenue
New York, New York 10165
(212) 371-9400

Chef Institutional Magazine
134 Main Street
New Canaan, Connecticut 06840
(203) 972-3022

Chicago Sun-Times
401 North Wabash Avenue
Chicago, Illinois 60611-3532
(312) 321-3000

Chicago Tribune
435 North Michigan Avenue
Chicago, Illinois 60611
(312) 222-3232

Club Management
408 Olive Street
St. Louis, Missouri 63102
(314) 421-5445

Consumer Reports
P.O. Box 53016
Boulder, Colorado 80322
(800) 525-0643

Convenience Store News
245 West 31st Street
New York, New York 10001
(212) 594-4120

Cornell Hotel and Restaurant Administration Quarterly
327 Statler Hall
Ithaca, New York 14853-0223
(607) 255-5093

Crain's Chicago Business
740 North Rush
Chicago, Illinois 60611
(800) 621-6877 ext. 5384

Financial World
P.O. Box 10750
Des Moines, Iowa 50340
(800) 666-6639

Food and Beverage Marketing
345 Park Avenue South
New York, New York 10010
(212) 686-7744

Food Distributors Magazine
1002 South Fort Harrison
Clearwater, Florida 34616
(813) 443-2723

FDA (Food and Drug Administration) Consumer
5600 Fishers Lane
Rockville, Maryland 20857
(301) 443-3170

Food Industry Futures
Box 430
Fayetteville, New York 13066
(315) 682-7455

Food Institute Report
28-12 Broadway
Fairlawn, New Jersey 07410
(201) 791-5570

Food Management
1 East First Street
Duluth, Minnesota 55802
(216) 826-2867

Food Production / Management
2619 Maryland Avenue
Baltimore, Maryland 21218
(301) 467-3338

Food-Service East
755 Boylston Street
Boston, Massachusetts 02116
(617) 267-9080

Foodservice Equipment Specialist
P.O. Box 5080, 1350 East Touhy Avenue
Des Plaines, Illinois
(312) 635-8800

Foodservice and Hospitality
980 Yonge Street, Suite 400
Toronto, Ontario M4W 2J8, Canada
(416) 932-8888

Forbes
60 Fifth Avenue
New York, New York 10011
(212) 620-2200

Fortune
541 North Fairbanks Court
Chicago, Illinois 60611
(800) 621-8200

Frozen Food Age
230 Park Avenue
New York, New York 10069
(212) 697-4727

Frozen Food Digest
271 Madison Avenue
New York, New York 10016
(212) 557-8600

Frozen Food Executive
P.O. Box 398
Hershey, Pennsylvania 17033
(717) 534-1601

The Gallagher Report
230 Park Avenue
New York, New York 10017
(212) 661-5000

Grocery Distribution Magazine
307 North Michigan Avenue, Room 924
Chicago, Illinois 60601
(312) 263-1057

Hotel and Motel Management
1 East First Street
Duluth, Minnesota 55802
(218) 723-9200

Hotel and Resort Industry
488 Madison Avenue
New York, New York 10022
(212) 888-1500

Hotels and Restaurants International
Cahner's Publishing Company
44 Cook Street
Denver, Colorado 80206
(303) 388-4511

*IFMA (International Foodservice Manufacturers
Assn.) News*
P.O. Box 395
Wheaton, Illinois 60189
(312) 682-9270

Illinois Foodservice News
350 West Ontario, 7th Floor
Chicago, Illinois 60610
(312) 787-4000

Journal of the American Dietetic Association
208 South LaSalle Street, Suite 1100
Chicago, Illinois 60604-1003
(312) 899-0040

Journal of Home Economics
American Home Economics Association
2010 Massachusetts Avenue NW
Washington, D. C. 20036-1028
(202) 862-8300

Journal of Marketing
American Marketing Association
250 South Wacker Drive, Suite 200
Chicago, Illinois 60606
(312) 648-0536

Lodging Hospitality
1111 Superior Avenue
Cleveland, Ohio 44114
(216) 696-7000

Los Angeles Times
Times Mirror Square
Los Angeles, California 90053
(213) 237-5000

Market Chronicle
45 John Street, Suite 911
New York, New York 10038
(212) 233-5200

Marketing News
American Marketing Association
250 South Wacker Drive, Suite 200
Chicago, Illinois 60606
(312) 648-0536

Monday Report on Retailers
777 Bay Street
Toronto, Ontario M5W 1A7, Canada
(416) 596-5939

National Provisioner
15 West Huron
Chicago, Illinois 60610
(312) 944-3380

NRA (National Restaurant Association) News
311 First Street NW
Washington, D.C. 20001
(202) 638-6100

Nation's Business
P.O. Box 2886
Boulder, Colorado 80322-2886
(800) 525-0643

Nation's Restaurant News
425 Park Avenue
New York, New York 10022
(212) 371-9400

Newsweek
1517 Microlab Road
Livingston, New Jersey 07039
(800) 631-1040

New York Times
229 West 43rd Street
New York, New York 10036-3913
(212) 556-1234

Onboard Services Magazine
665 La Villa Drive
Miami Springs, Florida 33166
(305) 887-1701

Prepared Foods Magazine
8750 West Bryn Mawr Avenue
Chicago, Illinois 60631
(312) 693-3200

Private Label Magazine
80 Eighth Avenue, Suite 801
New York, New York 10011
(212) 989-1101

Progressive Grocer
1351 Washington Boulevard
Stamford, Connecticut 06902
(203) 325-3500

Restaurant Business
633 Third Avenue
New York, New York
(212) 986-4800

Restaurant Hospitality
111 Superior Avenue
Cleveland, Ohio 44114
(216) 696-7000

Restaurant and Hotel Design
633 Third Avenue
New York, New York 10017
(212) 986-4800

Restaurants and Institutions
Cahner's Publishing Company
44 Cook Street
Denver, Colorado 80206
(303) 388-4511

Sales and Marketing Management
633 Third Avenue
New York, New York 10017
(212) 986-4800

School Food Service Journal
5600 South Quebec Street
Englewood, Colorado 80111
(800) 525-8575

School Food Service Research Review
5600 South Quebec Street
Englewood, Colorado 80111
(800) 525-8575

Seafood Business Report
21 Elm Street
Camden, Maine 04843
(207) 236-4342

Southeast Food Service News
P.O. Box 29823
Atlanta, Georgia 30359
(404) 452-1807

Supermarket News
Fairchild Publications
7 East 12th Street
New York, New York 10003
(800) 247-2160

Time, Inc.
541 North Fairbanks Court
Chicago, Illinois 60611
(800) 621-8200

U.S. News and World Report
P.O. Box 2886
Boulder, Colorado 80322
(800) 525-0643

Vending Times
545 Eighth Avenue
New York, New York 10018
(212) 714-0101

Wall Street Journal
200 Burnett Road
Chicopee, Maine 01021
(413) 592-7761

Western Foodservice
104 Fifth Avenue, 3rd Floor
New York, New York 10011
(212) 206-7440

Index